I0160466

G.E.M. ANSCOMBE AND HUMAN DIGNITY

Published by the
NEUMANN UNIVERSITY PRESS

Neumann University
One Neumann Drive
Aston, Pennsylvania 19104-1298

http://www.neumann.edu/

 | ISBN 978-1-944769-16-1

G.E.M. ANSCOMBE AND HUMAN DIGNITY

Edited by John Mizzoni

Table of Contents

Part 1

Introduction

1. The Anscombe Forum on Human Dignity

John Mizzoni

On March 13-14, 2015, my Neumann University colleagues and I hosted a conference on Neumann's campus that explored the work of G.E.M. Anscombe as it relates to the subject of human dignity. In the year prior, we initiated the Anscombe Forum with a conference on the topic of Anscombe's contributions to the Catholic intellectual tradition. At the 2014 Anscombe Forum, the conference participants examined a wide range of themes from Anscombe's work, including personhood, the soul, the will, and the doctrine of double effect, among other topics. Some papers explored how Anscombe's Catholic faith influenced her approach to philosophy and how her Catholic faith influenced the types of philosophical issues with which she dealt.[1]

---

[1] Select papers from the 2014 Anscombe Forum were published as *G.E.M. Anscombe and the Catholic Intellectual Tradition*, (eds.) John Mizzoni, Philip Pegan, and Geoffrey Karabin, (Aston, PA: Neumann University Press, 2016).

The papers in the present volume explore the concept of human dignity. Part II examines the nature of human dignity, with special focus on Anscombe's perspective, while the papers in Part III proceed to explore the implications of human dignity for doing applied ethics, specifically regarding the issues of euthanasia, physician-assisted suicide, abortion, and physical disability.

I thank the presenters at the 2015 Anscombe Forum for contributing to the conference and contributing their finalized papers to this volume. I also thank the chairs of the conference sessions,[2] the staff of Neumann University,[3] and Gerard O'Sullivan, formerly the Vice President for Academic Affairs at Neumann, who provided much support for both Anscombe Forums.

The plenary speaker at the 2015 Anscombe Forum was Duncan Richter, the author of *Anscombe's Moral Philosophy* (2010).[4] In Richter's paper below, "The Meaning of Human Dignity," which opens Part II on the nature of human dignity, Richter argues that Anscombe's work can help shed light on the topic of human dignity. He first surveys the idea of human dignity as understood by John Stuart Mill, Ludwig Wittgenstein, and Elizabeth Anscombe. He then discusses Anscombe's understanding of connatural knowledge as it relates to human dignity.

Richter continues by looking at some issues in applied ethics that Anscombe discusses in connection with the notion of human dignity—euthanasia, abortion, capital punishment, sex, and same-sex marriage. Following that, Richter discusses

[2]Philip Pegan, Geoffrey Karabin, and John Kruse.

[3]Especially Susan Long and Lee Strofe.

[4]Duncan Richter, *Anscombe's Moral Philosophy* (Lanham, MD: Lexington Books, 2010). Richter is also the author of *Ethics after Anscombe: Post "Modern Moral Philosophy"* (Kluwer, 2000), among other works.

a contemporary account of dignity (Rosen 2012).[5] Richter contends that to understand what human dignity means we need to think not only about words and concepts but about behavior—the application of these concepts in our lives. He reaches the conclusion that "consideration of practical cases can shed light on the notion of human dignity, and that consideration of human dignity can shed light on practical cases, but that neither provides a key for knowing with certainty what we ought to do in every practical case."

Candace Vogler, author of a forthcoming volume on the work of Anscombe, was the keynote speaker at the 2015 Anscombe Forum.[6] In her keynote address, Vogler discusses Anscombe's views about the value of human life. For Anscombe, human beings can be homely, disordered, and awful, says Vogler. Human beings have a fallen nature; and original sin is part of our physical inheritance. Anscombe believes that we can do something about our disorderly lives, however. We can change ourselves and decide how we should live. This shows something special about us. For Anscombe, human beings are created by God and seek a union with God. There is a sanctity to human life and we should revere human life as such.

---

[5]Michael Rosen, *Dignity: Its History and Meaning* (Cambridge, MA: Harvard University Press, 2012).

[6]Vogler was also our keynote speaker for the 2014 Anscombe Forum. Vogler's forthcoming volume on Anscombe is to be published by Routledge in its *Routledge Philosophers* series, a major series of introductions to the great Western philosophers. Vogler is also the author of: "G.E.M. Anscombe," in *The International Encyclopedia of Ethics*, (ed.) Hugh LaFollette, (Wiley-Blackwell, 2013); "Modern Moral Philosophy Again: Isolating the Promulgation Problem," *Proceedings of the Aristotelian Society* (2006); and "Anscombe on Practical Inference," in *Varieties of Practical Reasoning*, (ed.) Elijah Millgram, (MIT Press, 2001), among many other works. Most recently, Vogler was named Principal Investigator in a project funded by the John Templeton Foundation that will examine "Virtue, Happiness, and the Meaning of Life."

Through God's acts, we can know these truths about the value of human life, says Vogler. Yet formulating an account of the sanctity of human life that does not make reference to divinity is a more difficult task, she cautions. However, Vogler explains that by drawing from Aquinas "on human nature, natural law, and pagan virtue" we can "begin to have some resources to say why it is that we should have reverence for our fellow human beings even without adverting to theological accounts of our place in creation."

The next paper, by Bryan Pilkington, explores the Christian account of dignity defended by Gilbert Meilaender. Anscombe's insight about the respect we should have for noncombatants would seem to lead us in the direction of identifying the essential aspects of dignity, thinks Pilkington. As Pilkington argues however, dignity is a complex concept. There are meritorious elements of dignity, but also egalitarian elements of dignity. Pilkington argues that both aspects are needed. In addition, Pilkington observes a difference between human dignity and personal dignity. Because of the complexity of the concept of dignity, it is not surprising to Pilkington that there have been so many challenges to the concept of dignity, both its religious and non-religious versions.

After a detailed investigation of Meilaender's attempt to bring together the different aspects of dignity, Pilkington concludes that Meilaender's account is not an ultimately coherent account of dignity.

From Anscombe's writings, it is clear that she upholds a religious interpretation of dignity, for she has written that we ought to have "respect for that dignity of human nature so wonderfully created by God."[7] Hershenov's paper opens part III, on human dignity and applied ethics, and he examines two

[7]G.E.M. Anscombe, "The Dignity of the Human Being," in *Human Life, Action and Ethics: Essays by G.E.M. Anscombe*, (eds.) Mary Geach & Luke Gormally, (Exeter: Imprint Academic, 2005), p. 72.

non-religious accounts of dignity: Velleman's and Dworkin's. With their theories of human dignity, Velleman and Dworkin propose to justify euthanasia and physician assisted suicide. Hershenov, though, determines that both accounts of dignity are unsatisfactory in identifying what dignity really is. Hershenov claims to "argue instead for an account of dignity more in line with the tradition that Anscombe belonged to, where our value depends upon the kind of entity we are and thus what ends we ought to realize."

In the next essay, Cavanaugh also takes a position in line with Anscombe. In Anscombe's view, voluntary active euthanasia (VAE) cannot be supported by an appeal to the dignity of human freedom, even though advocates of VAE commonly attempt to do so. Cavanaugh agrees with Anscombe that such actions are really inconsistent with the dignity of self-rule.

Cavanaugh further describes a common claim of advocates of VAE: they assert that we treat dogs and cats better than we treat humans, because we are more inclined to euthanize our pets than human beings. "Do we treat our pets better than our fellow humans as they lay dying?" Cavanaugh asks. No, he argues. He discusses at least four good reasons that undermine the analogy of pet-euthanasia with person-euthanasia. While pet-euthanasia can be ethically justified, person-euthanasia cannot, he argues. Human dignity makes an important difference. Cavanaugh supports the position—as he thinks Anscombe would also—that those who employ the experience of pet-euthanasia to make a case for the supposed humaneness of VAE, in fact trivialize the gravity of homicide.

Ryan Cobb next examines Anscombe's argument against abortion, which uses the concept of human dignity. Cobb tries to make the reasoning in Anscombe's argument more explicit. A premise in Anscombe's argument is that violations of human dignity are morally wrong. Cobb tries to spell out why this is so; part of his strategy is to describe various examples of violations of human dignity. He presses the point that violations of human dignity are not necessarily violations of autonomy. Additionally, by focusing on the example of sex-selective abortions, Cobb seeks to rebut several possible objections to Anscombe's argument against abortion.

In the last paper of the volume, David DiQuattro investigates several of Anscombe's statements about human dignity. DiQuattro notes that Anscombe emphasizes the dignity of human beings, not only the dignity of *persons*. The view that *only* persons possess dignity DiQuattro calls the personhood account of dignity, and he argues that it is tied to a consequentialist ethical approach with which Anscombe disagrees. DiQuattro seeks to "bring out the insights Anscombe's work holds for thinking about physical handicap and genetic testing."

Overall, the essays reflect the difficulty, complexity, yet importance of the concept of human dignity. The essays also attest to the significance of the concept of dignity for many different kinds of ethical issues. Finally, by describing and in some cases defending both Anscombe's incisive perspective and her moral commitment, they convey Anscombe's important contributions to our understanding of the value of a human life.

Part 2

On the Nature of Dignity

2. The Meaning of Human Dignity

Duncan Richter

It is very difficult to say much about human dignity, but it seems worthwhile to try. I think that Anscombe's work can help to shed light on the topic, especially through her recognition that we are both rational and embodied beings, through what she says about connatural knowledge, and through her comments on several specific issues in practical ethics. What follows is divided into four main parts: an initial survey of the idea of human dignity, a brief discussion of connatural knowledge, a look at some relevant issues in applied ethics, and a final investigation of what it means to respect human dignity. My conclusion will be that consideration of practical cases can shed light on the notion of human dignity, and that consideration of human dignity can shed light on practical cases, but neither provides a key for knowing with certainty what we ought to do in every practical case.

I. Human Dignity

A certain respect seems proper to human beings. It is often thought that this has to do with the intellectual and moral powers that typical members of our species possess. John Stuart Mill refers to:

> a sense of dignity, which all human beings possess in one form or other, and in some, though by no means in exact, proportion to their higher faculties, and which is so essential a part of the happiness of those in whom it is strong, that nothing which conflicts with it could be, otherwise than momentarily, an object of desire to them. (1993, pp. 9-10)

As Mill sees it, in one sense we know the superiority of our own, higher mode of existence by acquaintance. We know both, he suggests, what it is like to be wise and what it is like to be a fool, and we know that it is better to be wise. If a fool thinks otherwise it is because he only knows what it is like to be a fool. So greater knowledge leads us to prefer the life of a human being to the life of a pig. But in another sense we just do happen to desire this mode of existence, so it is a matter of arbitrary preference, not something grounded in knowledge. We desire it because it is such an essential part of our happiness. And this does not mean that it *causes* happiness as an effect. It *constitutes* our happiness, or an important part of it at least. A sense of dignity makes us unwilling to exchange a 'higher' manner of existence for another that might make us more content.

As Thomas Nagel has pointed out, there is something wrong with the idea that a human being knows what it is like to be a bat or a pig. A Nietzschean might add that human beings are bound to regard themselves as better than other species, but that it does not follow that this belief is anything other than fiction.

On the other hand, it is hard to dismiss Mill's view completely. There is something nightmarish about the idea of choosing to become a fool or a pig simply for an increase in contentment. And it does seem that having experienced the pleasures of listening to good music or doing good deeds not only *inclines* us to prefer a life in which we enjoy such pleasures but also *educates* us about their value. This is relevant for the idea of connatural knowledge, which I will come to soon.

There is more to being human, though, than exercising the higher faculties. Indeed, it can seem that much lower considerations are really what is relevant. In a passage that has become well known, George Orwell says that he could not shoot at a man holding up his trousers:

> I had come here [viz., to Spain] to shoot at 'Fascists'; but a man who is holding up his trousers isn't a 'Fascist', he is visibly a fellow-creature, similar to yourself, and you don't feel like shooting at him. (Orwell, n.d.)

Being a fellow-creature in Orwell's sense does not require having higher faculties. In this case the fellowship is made visible by the man's holding up his trousers. One might try to argue that this is symptomatic of other capacities, but I think that would be a stretch. That is, it would be a stretch to take holding up one's trousers as essentially connected to rationality or having free will. Trouser-wearing itself, though, is clearly not what is essential here either. What matters is that the man holding up his trousers is the same kind of being as we are, one who lives the same kind of life as we do. What this amounts to would be hard to say precisely, and so Orwell's point might seem vague and unpersuasive. But if we do not accept that Orwell has made the point sufficiently, Wittgenstein (1993) gives additional reasons to connect human dignity with lower, more physical aspects of our being:

> Mutilate a human being all the way, cut off his arms & legs nose & ears & then see what remains of his self-respect & of his dignity & to what extent his concepts of such things still remain the same. We have no idea how these concepts depend on the ordinary, normal, condition of our body. What becomes of them when we are led by a leash with a ring through our tongues & tied-up? How much of a human being then remains in him? Into what sort of state does such a human being sink? We don't know that we are standing on a high & narrow rock & around us chasms in which everything looks completely different. (1993, pp. 147-148)

Wittgenstein appears to believe that he knows what would happen to a person in such circumstances, or at any rate to that person's idea of dignity and self-respect. Presumably there is a high risk that they would lose some self-respect. If they did not they would surely have to base their self-respect on something other than their physical appearance. Certainly other people are likely to lose respect for people who are badly mutilated or treated like animals. This is partly why sadistic prison guards sometimes treat people in this kind of way. Part of how we think about ourselves and others, Wittgenstein seems to be saying, depends on our not living like this. Our concepts depend on how we live, and vice versa.

It is not merely that our respect for others and ourselves depends on the condition of our bodies. Wittgenstein's claim is that the *concept* of human dignity depends on the normal condition of the body. To the extent that we are made more into an object, a helpless thing, and the extent to which we are treated like animals, led around on a leash, we lose not only self-respect but also our grip on the concept of human dignity, on its applicability to human beings. And yet this concept is extremely important. Without it we risk not only entering a world in which everything looks completely *different*. We risk entering a chasm or abyss. This, I believe, was a very real fear for Anscombe, as we will see when we look at her thoughts on legal abortion.

She identifies several aspects of "the worth and dignity of being human" (Anscombe, 2005b, p. 68). Part of it is having free will and being answerable for one's actions, the kind of consideration emphasized by Kant. Another part is bodily integrity, the kind of thing that Wittgenstein brings up. We are, as Anscombe (2005b) points out, "intellectual animals" (p. 70), with a bodily life. For this reason, to make "a vile spectacle" (Anscombe, 2005b, p. 69) of someone, as happens in the more grisly forms of capital punishment, is also to offend against human dignity.[1] We are moral beings, and we are embodied beings. Human dignity can be offended against by an attack on either aspect of human being.

II. Connatural Knowledge

Being human gives us a certain inside perspective on what respect for human dignity requires. This is where connatural knowledge comes in. St. Thomas Aquinas (1920) writes that:

> rectitude of judgment is twofold: first, on account of perfect use of reason, secondly, on account of a certain connaturality with the matter about which one has to judge. Thus, about matters of chastity, a man after inquiring with his reason forms a right judgment, if he has learnt the science of morals, while he who has the habit of chastity judges of such matters by a kind of connaturality. (1920: II-II, q. 45, article 2)

Having the virtue of chastity involves not merely knowing about the value of chastity but also caring about it. Because one's character has been shaped by, and into, the relevant

[1]See also Deuteronomy 25:3.

habit, one is sensitive to, and appreciative of, what is chaste and equally sensitive, and averse, to what is unchaste.

This can be a difficult idea to grasp. Catherine Green (2002) has noted that, "The notion of connaturality in practical knowledge, as discussed by both Jacques Maritain and Yves R. Simon, is intuitively attractive," but that, "the language used by both Maritain and Simon to describe such knowledge is poetic, a-rational and obscure" (p. 43). Anscombe's account of the idea is down to earth and intuitive. She makes a distinction between knowledge of what she calls "indifferent truth" and connatural knowledge, knowledge of non-indifferent truth (Anscombe, 2005a, p. 59). Connatural knowledge inclines us to do, or not do, acts of certain kinds. "One might," she writes, "compare this to the revulsion which is sometimes part of the perception of something as disgusting, as, for example, if someone were to spit into one's glass" (Anscombe, 2005a, p. 60). Connatural knowledge often comes from virtue, so that a generous person will perceive the meanness of an action and so be inclined against it even without forming a judgment that the act in question is mean.

Patterns of behaviour and psychology give us insight into other matters not always recorded in books. But it does not have to come from virtue. Anscombe (2005a) gives as examples "the knowledge that a human being is of more worth than many sparrows" and that "it is wickedness ... to value making money far above respecting the lives of human infants" (p. 62) (she refers here to the reported campaign by the Nestlé Company to persuade women in Africa to feed babies powdered milk instead of their own). Connatural knowledge, non-indifferent knowledge, she suggests, comes from "experience of life, of suffering, and above all of moral practice" (Anscombe, 2005a, p. 64). That there is a kind of knowledge like this is a widespread belief, but of course it is hard to prove. It is not what we are used to being told counts as knowledge. And so far as it takes virtue to perceive certain truths then the vicious will be blind to them.

Consider the example of respecting the lives of human infants. Nestlé has been boycotted on and off over the years. Arguably powdered milk is less healthy than breast milk. It certainly is in places where there is no clean water with which to mix the powdered milk. In their book *Poor Economics*, Abhijit V. Banerjee and Esther Duflo (2011) point out that, "exclusive breast-feeding until six months" has been proven effective in combatting diarrhea, which kills nearly two million children under five years old each year (p. 47).[2] So encouraging the use of powdered milk seems unhelpful at best. Aggressively marketing a product that people can ill-afford in less developed countries is also questionable.

Against this line of thought it might be urged that Nestlé is not forcing anyone to do anything, and that providing people with more options for feeding their babies is surely a good thing. At this point a utilitarian calculus suggests itself as the obvious way to settle the dispute. But another response is to tell the Nestlé-sympathizer to come off it. Experience of life, especially experience of caring for babies, is likely to make the superficially plausible pro-business argument smell pretty rotten. Experience of moral practice is likely to be relevant too. If we know first-hand what doing the right thing and trying to do the right thing, and what trying to avoid wrong-doing, are like, then we will likely detect the shallowness and implausibility of the pro-Nestlé argument in this case without the need for a calculation of expected utility. Indeed performing such a calculation might lend more respect to the pro-Nestlé argument than it deserves.

[2]The figure of nearly two million is based on their assertion on p. 42 that nine million children die each year before their fifth birthday and that "roughly one in five" of these dies of diarrhea.

Utilitarians might claim to deny that we should care about anything so obscure or religious-sounding as human dignity, but Mill would not, many other philosophers also agree that human beings have a special dignity, and perhaps we *all* agree on this. Anscombe (2005b) says that this dignity is violated by the deliberate killing of a fetus in abortion, which many people will not accept, but she also says that it is violated by someone "who puts his dead or dying mother out into a rubbish bin" (p. 68). Everyone will surely agree that this kind of behaviour is an offense against humanity.

But even if we all agree that human dignity exists and ought to be respected, we do not agree on what this means in practice. Whatever one thinks of the ethics of abortion, for example, it is rarely regarded as insane, whereas the man who puts his dying mother in a trash can has surely lost his mind. Killing a fetus is a nasty business that some regard as necessary or the lesser of two evils in certain cases. Disposing of the dead like trash seems more like part of an appalling farce, unless it were to become the norm, in which case it might be a scene from hell or a dystopia. A case could be made, however, that we are already living in a kind of hell. Anscombe (2005b) claimed that, because of liberal abortion laws, we live in "a nation of murderers" (p. 73). Most people probably do not see our nation that way, but it would be superficial to reject her view merely for this reason. Instead I think it is worthwhile to look more closely at what she says about abortion and other matters of practical ethical concern. This might help us to see what respect for human dignity requires.

III. Practical Ethics

In the next few paragraphs I will look briefly at some issues in practical ethics that Anscombe mentions in connection with the idea of human dignity, starting with euthanasia and capital punishment. I will not be able to say much about any of these issues, but my hope is that each will shed some light on the central question of what human dignity is and means. Anscombe regards active non-voluntary euthanasia and abortion as crimes against human dignity in a way that capital punishment is not. Not that she supports capital punishment. Her point is more that one can support capital punishment while still maintaining respect for human persons. To think that someone deserves to die is to think of that person as a moral being, a responsible and autonomous being. This is true even if one is quite wrong (morally) and acts outside the law in order to get revenge. Execution is not an act that treats the person being punished as a mere object, as something in the way. Non-voluntary euthanasia, though, might be that kind of act, if done to free up a hospital bed, for instance. Even voluntary euthanasia could perhaps be chosen by someone who thinks of himself as little or nothing more than an obstacle to other people and their ability to live as they want. Anscombe (2005b) compares non-voluntary euthanasia with murder on the basis that in each case the victim "is to be killed because of the 'disvalue' of his life; his living is of negative value and so things are better with him dead" (p. 69). Of course she does not mean that things are *actually* better with this person dead. She is expressing the point of view of the killer. The negative value of this person's life, I take it she means, is negative for other people. Voluntary euthanasia, however much we might oppose it, is presumably (hopefully) usually chosen for the sake of the person to be killed. Non-voluntary euthanasia of the kind Anscombe has in mind is chosen for the sake of others. The patient or victim is treated essentially as an obstacle, as a thing.

At the other end of human life, human dignity is relevant also to the ethics of abortion. There is almost universal agreement that abortion is bad. What we do not agree about is whether it is ever the acceptably lesser of two evils. And what is bad about it, we might also agree, is its going against human dignity. Abortion treats a fetus as a kind of obstacle, if not a mere thing then at least something closer to a thing than a true human being. And this is indeed similar to what someone does who puts a dying man in a bin.

Not only matters of life and death but also questions of sexual ethics can be related to the idea of human dignity. As "intellectual animals," Anscombe (2005b) writes, reason and love enter into all "characteristically human" exercises of sexual activity (pp. 70-71). Sex that is both mindless and loveless is animal, as I think many people would agree even if they do not share Anscombe's moral views. We might not be able to escape our animality, but we do not have to aim for or celebrate being merely animal. Anscombe (2005b) says that we "violate human dignity by not respecting human sexuality" (p. 71), as for instance when we use artificial means to create new human life. This is not a matter of sinking to the level of beasts but of treating humanity as something like just another part of the physical universe, to be manipulated and brought into being by any means that work. "If we do this," she writes, "if we don't stick to human procreation of human beings, we generate further contempt for beginning human life and further alienation from belief in the dignity and value of human-ness" (Anscombe, 2005b, p. 72).

She objects to same-sex marriage on related grounds. The dignity and value of human-ness combined with the fact that we reproduce sexually counts strongly for her against homosexual sex. Artificial procreation allegedly disrespects human sexuality by reproducing without sex, while homosexual sex allegedly disrespects it by engaging in a kind of sex that cannot lead to reproduction. In each case there is a separation or decoupling, if I may make a pun, of sex from reproduction. This is convenient and helps us get what we want, but perhaps at the cost of failing to honour the natural order sufficiently. There might also be unintended consequences that we do not like, such as a reduced sense of the preciousness of life or an increase in casualness and perhaps commodification in our sex lives. Anscombe cares both about the violation of human dignity that she sees in such acts and the bad effects that she sees them as having. The latter kind of concern is an empirical matter that I am not well placed to judge, however, so I will focus on the question of whether human dignity is violated in such a practice as same-sex marriage.

Whether it is depends at least in part on what marriage is. One view of marriage, which I take to be Anscombe's, is that it is essentially connected with the getting and raising of children. Couples who do not intend to have children and those who know that they cannot have children might still get married, partly because their intentions or what they had thought they knew might change, and partly because of the very close resemblance between a childless heterosexual marriage and heterosexual marriage with children. A homosexual marriage, it might be argued, is simply too different to count as a real marriage. Heterosexual couples can also be biologically incapable of having children, but not in quite the same way. Vasectomies can fail to achieve the desired effect, and they can be reversed, for instance. But the impossibility of pregnancy is more radical for same-sex couples. Perhaps, therefore, same-sex marriage is wrong. An argument such as this, depending on degrees of similarity to a paradigm, has obvious limits to its ability to persuade. It is not thereby illegitimate, but I see no way to determine whether it is sound.

Anscombe suggests that all sexual acts of the kind that cannot lead to pregnancy go against human dignity. A case along these lines might be made if such acts treat human beings as mere objects, and if the kind of sexual act that can lead to pregnancy involves treating people in a way that is significantly different from this. But it is not clear how we are to make out what does or does not treat someone as a mere object. Whether mutual masturbation, to use one of Anscombe's examples, can respect human dignity is, it seems to me, a matter of perception (see Anscombe, 1981, p. 96). It seems as clear to me that it can as it does to her that it cannot. As far as reason, love, and the avoidance of both the bestial and the machinelike go, mutual masturbation seems to me to be a possibly rational and loving solution to the problem that Anscombe imagines of a couple's not being able to have the kind of sex that she approves of as a result of injuries sustained in an accident. There is, I think, a danger that "mutual stimulation" might become a little too mechanical, a little too different from anything that might involve a meeting of hearts or minds. Reason and love belong in human sexual relations, as Anscombe says, and there is a real danger of the absence of both when sex becomes too purely biological, too much simply a matter of dealing with urges by the most convenient means possible. I think, that is to say, that Anscombe has a point and that I appreciate this point. But the point does not seem as strong to me as it does to her. I do not know how to decide which of us is misperceiving the truth, though, beyond appeal to public opinion. I think that it is on my side, but perhaps that just shows how corrupt our society is. Knowing what is required by due respect for humanity involves knowledge of non-indifferent truth. When we disagree about such matters this might be because of differences in virtue or experience. Philosophical argument offers little hope of resolving differences of this kind.

IV. Respect for Human Dignity

What appears to be the case regarding both who or what is owed the respect required by human dignity and what such respect requires is that there is some sort of standard, or perhaps standards, and then a shadow or penumbra about which there is disagreement that is hard to resolve. As far as the question of who has human dignity goes the obvious answer is something like: people like you and me. Most of us would include both the recently dead and those about to be born among those who should be treated with a special kind of respect, but we disagree about how much respect is owed in the first stages of human life and to the remains of people who have been dead for a long time. Similarly we agree that non-consensual sex is an offense against human dignity, but we disagree about whether contraception, say, is offensive in the same way. I think we agree that it is not offensive in the same degree, but some see it as wrong and others as perfectly all right. If we could identify the basis of the respect in question then the right view might become clearer.

In contrast to what I have just said about the standard and the penumbra, Andrew Gleeson (2014), in his review of Michael Rosen's book *Dignity* (2012), argues that, "an approach in terms of paradigm valuable adult humans, natural as it might seem, goes wrong in at least two ways" (p. 371). His first complaint is that it matters that human beings can love, be brave or humble, and can feel grief or remorse (this list is not meant to be exhaustive). These capacities seem especially relevant to our sense of what gives moral significance to human life. A being incapable of virtue and of characteristically moral feelings would not be an obvious candidate for a paradigm of the bearer of value no matter how rational or sentient it might be. Secondly, he complains that if we are talking about who or what has value then it "begs the question" against the weak, the defenceless, the dependent, and the vulnerable if we start with a relatively independent and strong paradigm of human dignity (Gleeson, 2014, p. 371). Most of us would count the very young and the handicapped as having at least as much value as anyone else, and perhaps even as having special value precisely because of their vulnerability.

Gleeson's claim is not that the respect demanded by human dignity is owed to any being that can love, say, or that is defenceless. It is rather that a *human* life demands this kind of respect. We love and respect human beings, not certain of their qualities. Other lives, such as those of animals, do not demand such love and respect, but not because those lives lack specific features that human lives have. Rather, it *makes no sense* to treat animals the way we treat human beings. It would be ridiculous, indeed impossible, to do so. We cannot, for instance, bury an animal with great pomp and solemnity because the funeral's *being for an animal* would turn the pomp and solemnity into something else, something perhaps pompous but not solemn.

Cora Diamond (1991, pp. 351-352) has pointed out, though, that we can make different things out of the differences between human beings and members of other species. There are biological differences between men and women, and between human beings and members of other species. But there are also other differences, not discoverable empirically but rather "made by literature, art, and common thought and life over centuries" (Diamond, 1991, p. 351).[3] These differences, being created by human activity, can be altered by human activity. And so what makes sense given these differences can also change.

It is worth bearing in mind, too, that the differences between human beings and animals can be overstated. We do bury animals and mark their graves in ways that are not always ridiculous. We do love certain animals, and treat them with a measure of respect. Pets in particular have places in our lives that are both like and unlike the places occupied by human beings. It is not always, in every way, impossible or nonsensical to treat animals as we treat human beings. And the ways we treat animals could change, as could the ways we treat people, so that it is not too hard to imagine a day when both animal and human dead are disposed of in the same way. This might not be a good thing, for various reasons, but it is not as unimaginable as a square circle.

[3]She is talking specifically about the notion of difference-of-sex.

Nevertheless, there are important conceptual links between our nature as human beings and our respect for human dignity. Gleeson expands on this in response to a passage from Rosen's book. Rosen (2012) writes that:

> Our duty to respect the dignity of humanity is [...] fundamentally a duty toward ourselves. By which I mean, not that we are benefited when we observe our duties, but that our duties are so deep a part of us that we could not be the people that we are without having them. In failing to respect the humanity of others we actually undermine humanity in ourselves. (2012, p. 157)

Gleeson (2014) then comments that, "This is both very close to the truth and very distant from it" (p. 378). It is close, he says, because being the kind of being that we are depends on, or essentially involves, caring about others, or at the least being capable of caring for others, in such a way that we would never dispose of them like trash or an animal if they were to lose their rationality as the result of an accident. It is far from the truth, he adds, however, because of Rosen's implication that we can *justify* the respect we show humanity by reference to our own humanity, or, for that matter, by reference to anything else. We can to some extent explain, make sense of, our treatment of human beings. We do not relate to them as we do to animals and so we do not react to their deaths as we do to those of animals. But this does not, as Gleeson sees it, *justify* the different forms of treatment. Different attitudes do not justify different treatment. Rather they are reflected or expressed in it. We treat children and animals differently because we have different attitudes towards them and, at least in part, we have different attitudes because we treat them differently. The treatment embodies the attitudes that inform it. Neither justifies the other. And the attempt to justify a certain way of behaving with regard to children by referring to various properties that children have not only opens the door to outrageous treatment of children who happen to lack some of these properties and to absurd treatment of members of other species who might turn out to have them. It also fails to do conceptual justice to children as children, as beings of a particular kind with a particular kind of place in our lives rather than as advanced primates or mere bearers of properties. I think that Gleeson is right about this. Certainly he is right that my duties to others do not depend on my duties to myself, which are no greater or more fundamental than my duty to treat others with respect. Nor is regard for my own humanity a reason, or the *right* reason, for respecting the humanity of others.

Rosen sees that children are not dignified. Gleeson (2014) adds to this that babies are even less dignified, and that illness and age gradually strip us "of the qualities that go to constitute our dignity" (p. 381). And yet people like Rosen, who want to talk about human dignity, think of it as something that is inalienable. So there is a problem here: how can we reconcile the idea that we all, children included, have something called "human dignity" that we cannot lose with the idea that children lack dignity and all of us lose our dignity eventually, if we are lucky enough to live into old age? Gleeson's proposed solution is to talk instead of "our shared humanity, of bonds of quasi-familial love" (Gleeson, 2014, p. 382). This is something that is genuinely inalienable, he suggests. Anscombe (2005b) makes a similar point when she says that, "The equality of human beings in the worth and dignity of being human is one that can't be taken away, no matter how much it is violated. Violations remain *violations*" (p. 68).

There are multiple senses of 'dignity' at work in Gleeson's discussion of Rosen.[4] The dignity that babies, children, the

[4]Gleeson (2014) notes that: "Rosen distinguishes four main concepts of dignity: dignity as *status*, dignity as dignified *manner or bearing*, dignity as *intrinsic value*, and dignity as *respectful treatment*" (p. 365).

sick, and the dying lack is not dignity-as-intrinsic-value. Anyone who agrees that human beings, as distinct from rational beings, have intrinsic value will grant that babies have it too. Dignity-*as-intrinsic-value* is something they have. What Rosen calls dignity as dignified manner or bearing, they lack. This is a reason, as Gleeson argues, for talking about humanity rather than dignity. But we *can* lose not only the bonds of quasi-familial love but also our humanity itself. We can, after all, die, and although the dead are owed a certain respect, this fades with time.

Even while we are still alive, though, we can lose our humanity in an important sense. Perhaps if we replace enough of our bodies with robotic parts we will effectively die and cease to be human that way. This would be something like a less violent version of the assault on the body that Wittgenstein talks about. But we can also cease to be human by doing evil deeds. This damage to our humanity might not be irreparable (I don't know) but it can be done. Do we then lose our human worth? In one sense yes, but not in the sense that we lose our intrinsic value. And in that sense also we do not, cannot, lose our humanity. Even a man who deserves to be killed, if that is something it is possible to deserve, would not deserve to be killed like an animal. (Perhaps animals do not deserve that either.) As Anscombe reminds us, we are physical and moral beings, and we can, in different senses, lose our humanity through changes in our material being and through immorality. But as long as we *are* human, to some impossible-to-specify-minimally-necessary-extent, we deserve the respect that is owed to humanity.

Gleeson is influenced by Raimond Gaita, who addresses some of these issues in his book *A Common Humanity*. Gaita (2000) rejects secular talk of "inalienable dignity" because, he thinks, such forms of words are "ways of trying to make secure to reason what reason cannot fully underwrite" (p. 5). He also rejects religious talk of human sacredness because he thinks that the concept of sanctity lacks "a secure home outside" religious traditions (Gaita, 2000, p. 5). Instead he prefers talk about human beings, human fellowship, and love (se Gaita, 2000, p. 14). This is a circular approach, as I think Gaita would concede, because it makes no attempt to underwrite or justify such love and fellowship. Someone's being a human being, and not simply a member of the species *homo sapiens*, does not justify our treating him or her in this way or that. Rather, part of what it means to regard or think of another as a human being is that a certain kind of behaviour is appropriate and other kinds are not. These forms of behaviour are open-ended: it is impossible to specify all the acts that would be reasonable to do to or for another human being and all those that are off the table. But to understand the concept *human being* is to be able to behave accordingly, appropriately.[5] How we describe or understand what a thing is is not independent of "our active relation to it," as Gaita has put it elsewhere (Gaita, 2004, p. 122). His point is similar to Diamond's, perhaps not accidentally. We understand our world in terms of the concepts that we learn growing up, and these concepts are both learned in and apply to forms of practice. Knowing what a dog is involves knowing not only what the word 'dog' means, what kind of object it refers to, but also knowing what *dogs* mean, what place they have in people's lives. Knowing what a human being is involves not just some biology but understanding what belongs to human life.

The inviolability of human dignity, the sense in which our humanity is something that we cannot lose, is connected with the idea that certain forms of behaviour are off the table or simply out of the question. As long as we are dealing with a human being, certain types of actions must not be done to that human being. To say that we cannot lose our humanity is

[5]The ability I mean here is intellectual. A physical inability to do the right thing would not show a lack of understanding of what is called for.

to say, in part, that we cannot stop deserving a certain kind of treatment. Actions incompatible with such treatment are out of the question. They are violations.

The distinction between what is human and what is inhuman is in some ways like the distinction between sense and nonsense. Inhuman acts are unreasonable and in fact irrational. Not in the neo-Humean sense of being contrary to arbitrary goals set by the self for itself, but in another equally legitimate sense of the word 'irrational'. Putting a dying person out with the trash is madness. "Senseless slaughter" is indeed senseless. There is no limit to what lies outside the limit, if I can put the point that way, so we can never map what is out of bounds. Nor can we discover the essence of the irrational by looking for reasons why senseless behaviour is senseless, or regarded as such. Madness need have nothing in common except that it is not sane. And nonsense need have nothing in common either. It is nonsense because it is not sense, because it is excluded from what we do and say, like a coin that is not in currency.

I do not want to suggest though that good behaviour is simply what makes sense and bad is what does not make sense. We do have established practices that tell us, in some cases at least, what is right and what is wrong. For instance, if I have promised to meet you at 2 o'clock and I do not show up until 3 then I have broken my promise. I have acted wrongly so far as the promise is concerned, and unless I have a good excuse I have acted wrongly period. Breaking a promise can be both wrong and intelligible. Conversely, a good act can be hard to understand. People marvel at villagers who risked their lives to rescue Jews from Nazis, to give one perhaps over-familiar example.[6] The life of Jesus is another example, at which even Nietzsche marvelled. And Gaita (2000) writes about his work's being inspired by "a nun whose behaviour showed a

---

[6]I am thinking of the villagers of Le Chambon, discussed by Philip Hallie (1981).

goodness that" he found wondrous (p. 2). He says of her that, "It would be no fault in any account of ethics if it failed to find words to make fully intelligible what the nun revealed, for she revealed something mysterious" (Gaita, 2000, p. 19). So bad behaviour can be understood and good behaviour can be hard to fully comprehend. This challenges my suggestion that good behaviour is like sense and bad behaviour is like nonsense.

On the other hand, marvellous behaviour is not exactly unintelligible. Surprising perhaps, but not at all what we would call senseless. Only a cynic would describe it that way. And although promise-breaking is intelligible in the sense that it is all too human, we might still ask of a promise-breaker "How could you do that?" When an amazing new kind of behaviour, passive resistance, for example, occurs we instantly take it into our currency. Not, perhaps, as behaviour we are likely to go in for ourselves, but certainly as a form of currency that we will accept from others. The good need not be expected, but it is (when recognized as the good) welcomed. The bad, of course, is not. So there is, I think, a real analogy between what makes sense and what is good, on the one hand, and between evil and nonsense on the other. Good treatment of others makes sense given the concept *human being*, the idea of what a human being is that informs our lives. Bad treatment is treatment that fails to do so. But this concept itself cannot be justified in any absolute way. Nor can we specify exhaustively in advance what will or will not make sense to us.

V. Conclusion

So where does this leave us with regard to abortion, euthanasia, same-sex marriage and the rest? There are no easy answers. We cannot go from the obvious injustice of killing me now to an analysis of what properties such an act would have, to a prescription or proscription regarding other kinds of action. Of course we can draw analogies, but we can also dispute them. Justifications of all of these acts tend to be made on broadly utilitarian grounds, but I would strongly suggest that these should not be the *only* grounds we consider. The other grounds I have mentioned concern what makes sense and what it makes sense to regard as good. To some people these acts do make sense, to others they do not. Or at least they seem to do so. Perhaps an act, like a sentence, either makes sense or else does not, so that if people disagree then at least one of them must be wrong. If so, however, it is still not easy to see how to calculate or neutrally discover who is right. The same goes for regarding acts such as abortion and euthanasia as possibly, conceivably, good. It would be nonsense to call them good unless one meant something like the least bad course of action available in the circumstances. But it at least appears to be an intelligible thought that they *could* be the least evil of the options facing someone. Whether we should agree with this thought and accept abortion or euthanasia is another matter, but not one that I can give any advice about.

The idea of human dignity is deeply rooted in the way we think and live. So much so that the idea of giving it up, of going "beyond dignity", would be terrifying if it were not so hard to take seriously.[7] To understand what human dignity means we need to think not only about words or concepts but about behaviour, about the application of these concepts in our lives. This might sound like relativism, but I don't mean that whatever we do is thereby all right. Part of what we do, after all, is to condemn certain kinds of action as not all right. The question is one of compatibility or consistency. Is contraception compatible with respect for human dignity? If it is not perfectly or maximally

---

[7] I am echoing the title of Skinner (1971), but nothing I say is specifically about this book.

compatible with it, is it nevertheless compatible enough? This is the kind of question that I do not know how to answer. It might come down to faith in the end. Has the world been made such that it is possible for human beings to live lives that make sense, that do justice to all that is good? Are there tragic situations in which we must choose the lesser of two evils? I do not know.

References

Anscombe, G. E. M. (1981). You Can have Sex without Children: Christianity and the New Offer. In *Ethics, Religion and Politics: Collected Papers Volume III*, (82-96). Oxford: Basil Blackwell.

Anscombe, G. E. M. (2005a). Knowledge and Reverence for Human Life. In M. Geach and L. Gormally (Eds.), *Human Life, Action and Ethics: Essays by G. E. M. Anscombe*, (59-66). Exeter, UK: Imprint Academic.

Anscombe, G. E. M. (2005b). The Dignity of the Human Being. In M. Geach and L. Gormally (Eds.), *Human Life, Action and Ethics: Essays by G. E. M. Anscombe*, (67-73). Exeter, UK: Imprint Academic.

Aquinas, T. (1920) *The Summa Theologica of St. Thomas Aquinas*. Second and Revised Edition. Literally translated by Fathers of the English Dominican Province. Retrieved from http://www.newadvent.org/summa/

Banerjee, A. V. and Duflo, E. (2011). *Poor Economics: A Radical Rethinking of the Way to Fight Global Poverty*. New York: PublicAffairs.

Diamond, C. (1991). *The Realistic Spirit: Wittgenstein, Philosophy, and the Mind*. Cambridge, MA: MIT Press.

Gaita, R. (2000). *A Common Humanity: Thinking about Love and Truth and Justice*. London: Routledge.

Gaita, R. (2004). *Good and Evil: An Absolute Conception.* Second edition. New York: Routledge.

Gleeson, A. (2014). The Limits of Dignity. *Philosophical Investigations*, 37:4, 363-382.

Green, C. (2002). It Takes One to Know One: Connaturality—Knowledge or Prejudice? In Ollivant, D. A. (Ed.), *Jacques Maritain and the Many Ways of Knowing*, (43-55). Washington, D. C.: Catholic University of America Press.

Hallie, P. (1981). From Cruelty to Goodness. *Hastings Center Report*, 11, 23–28.

Mill, J. S. (1993). *Utilitarianism, On Liberty, Considerations on Representative Government, Remarks on Bentham's Philosophy*. London: Everyman.

Nagel, T. (1974). What is it like to be a Bat? *Philosophical Review*, *LXXXIII* (4), 435-450.

Orwell, G. (n. d.) Looking Back on the Spanish War. *Fifty Orwell Essays*. Retrieved from http://gutenberg.net.au/ebooks03/0300011h.html

Rosen, M. (2012). ***Dignity: Its History and Meaning***. Cambridge, MA: Harvard University Press.

Skinner, B. F. (1971). *Beyond Freedom and Dignity*. New York: Knopf.

Wittgenstein, L. (1993). *Philosophical Occasions, 1912-1951*. Indianapolis: Hackett Publishing.

3. Why Human Beings Matter: Anscombe on the Nature and Point of Human Life

Candace Vogler

In a radio talk given in 1957, Elizabeth Anscombe argued that the moral philosophy fashionable in Oxford in her day (deeply contrary to Catholic Intellectual Tradition) did not, in fact, corrupt the youth. In order to support a charge of corruption, she pointed out, one needs to show:

1. That the youth were on the road to good character before university;
2. That the moral philosophy promulgated through writings, tutorials, and lectures at Oxford could derail the developing good character of the youth; and
3. That Oxford moral philosophy was at odds with the kind of commonsense morality that shaped popular opinion and ordinary moral education—a commonsense morality that might otherwise serve as a source of correction for what the Oxford philosophers were saying.

None of these things were true. Ergo, the youth were *not* corrupted by Oxford moral philosophy. They were affirmed in the bad habits and bad judgments that were common as dirt in England.[1]

Anscombe recognized that human beings tend to be homely and disordered. This is part of why we love her, I think. She accepted significant aspects of Aquinas's teaching on original sin—that it was part of our physical inheritance rather than a disfiguration of our rational souls.[2]

Original sin deprived us of a kind of supernatural order—"original justice"— as Aquinas puts it. In the special circumstances of original justice, by grace, the human intellect was subordinate to God, and human will, emotions, and actions were subordinate to the intellect. The whole system had its clear source in God and was inclined to God. This was true of creation in general, on Aquinas's account, and original sin was a break with prelapsarian human nature.[3] The view has it that, because of original sin, we suffer from a darkened intellect, disturbed passions, and a disordered will. I take it that this just *is* the absence of the order that harmonizes our intellects, wills, and emotions—hearts and minds—in subordination to God. For those who are disinclined to believe in the theological framework, it may be no more than a concise description of how people tend to be.

---

[1]G. E. M. Anscombe, "Does Oxford Moral Philosophy Corrupt the Youth?", reprinted in Mary Geach and Luke Gormally, editors, *Human Life, Action and Ethics: Essays by G. E. M. Anscombe,* (Exeter: Imprint Academic, 2005), pp. 161-168.

[2]G. E. M. Anscombe, "The Early Embryo," in Mary Geach and Luke Gormally, editors, *Faith in a Hard Ground: Essays on Religion, Philosophy and Ethics by G. E. M. Anscombe*, (Exeter: Imprint Academic, 2008), pp. 222-223.

[3]My understanding of Aquinas on original sin is deeply indebted to P. De Letter's work on the topic. See De Letter, "Original Sin, Privation of Original Justice," *Thomist*, 17 (1954), pp. 484-485. De Letter stresses that original sin is a sin of nature, and that human nature can't be deprived of sanctifying grace because sanctifying grace is a gift to a person, not a gift to nature.

So *one* thing one might think about what makes human beings special is that we appear to be the only kind of organism around that has tremendous difficulty living in a way that it befits our kind of creature to live—to work for the common good when that will disrupt ruthless pursuit of private advantage, to work for long-term good when there is something very shiny we could try to get here and now, and so on. And in and through such things we have become animals capable of destroying the planet. That's special. No pod of dolphins, however clever, ever enjoyed any such horizon of practical possibility.

Anscombe spoke forcefully to the awfulness of human beings. For example, remarking how far short we fall of pursuing genuine human good and avoiding evil, she remarked:

> [When Christ was among us, all] over the world, almost, idolatry prevailed and awful laws and customs. And this is still so—at any rate, I am inclined to believe it, from the things which from time to time come to light. Certainly there are many millions of idolaters. I am on the whole not well-informed enough to give an account of the miseries and wickedness of mankind with chapter and verse cited in evidence. I don't suppose that I could do it for the circles that I am used to—the world of Anglo-American academic philosophy.[4]

She mentions that among mainstream academic philosophers—people who pride themselves on the routine rigorous and methodical exercise of rational powers—we see almost nothing of what might rightly be called matters illuminated by the natural light of human reason. They do not understand that there is any such thing as true morality or true religion, for example.

[4]G. E. M. Anscombe, "Sin," in *Faith in a Hard Ground*, p.153.

I take it that points like these explain why human beings should be feared. But the plain fact that we are very dangerous to ourselves, to one another, and everything else besides cannot account for why human life should be *revered*. On my reading at least, discussion of the dignity of human life in Anscombe tends to be tied fairly closely to an understanding that we should cultivate a lively sense of the sanctity of human life, in short, that we should have reverence for human life as such.

Toward Reverence for Human Life

To understand why Anscombe thought we should be revered, it helps to think a bit more about fallen human nature.[5] Rational appetite no longer effectively operates in and from practical wisdom subordinated to God. We impede ourselves. The corrective supplied by virtues like temperance, fortitude, justice, and prudence is meant to address the loss of the kind of governance proper to our natures, given the kind of creatures that we are, to begin to re-integrate our powers—or at least to foster cooperation among them—in a way that helps to rectify the will. If Aquinas is right, we only ever enjoyed the kind of order that it belongs to human nature to seek as a gift from God. And still we are creatures for whom it is possible to pursue human good and avoid human bad, creatures whose bits are (given the kinds of bits they are) inclined toward just that, whether or not the relevant powers develop and are exercised in just that way. On this view, given original sin, it is hard for us to manage even significant improvement. Anscombe thought that this was so even for most Christians. She wrote:

> Christianity is thoroughly conditioned by original sin. For that reason secular Christians—that is, Christians

---

[5] I am grateful to Jay Schleusener for pressing me on this point.

> who reside in the world, having property, pursuing the possibility of a happy life, perhaps marrying—are a pretty suspect sort of Christian.... It is true that we have nothing to do, absolutely nothing, but to keep the commandments in faith and in hope. There is not a lower sort of life, which is keeping the commandments, and a higher sort which is going three steps better than keeping the commandments, a life in which you do not just keep the commandments but do better, you observe the counsels of poverty, chastity, and obedience. No: but the truth is that those who do not observe the counsels are less likely to keep the commandments because they are less likely to be detached from the goods of the world.[6]

Keeping the commandments in faith and in hope is, she thinks, at the core of pursuing the good it belongs to human beings to pursue. She is not claiming that family life is contrary to human good. She is noticing that it is difficult to avoid being *of* the world when your primary attachments are to your family, your job, your worldly pleasures, and the need to satisfy your creditors. The faith and hope she mentions are Christian faith and the hope of salvation. She is working with a picture that is familiar to many of us in which human beings are created by God and seek a union with God. The teaching on original sin remains a teaching in which it is in our natures to seek an order in which reason governs our inclinations and actions, and reason itself is obedient to God. It is very hard for us to manage such a life. That we have to struggle, that disorderly psychological and practical lives belong to us, and that it is up to us to do something about that, is part of what sets us apart from other animals, on this view. And, for Anscombe, on my reading, it shows something of why human life has a special sort of dignity and requires a special sort of reverence.

---

[6] G. E. M. Anscombe, "On Attachment to Things and Obedience to God," in *Faith in a Hard Ground*, pp. 63-64.

Where human life, human good, and human psychology are concerned, we are to *start* from an understanding of the sanctity of human life rather than try to build up to it by meditating on the excellent things that people sometimes do, the excellent characters that some people cultivate, and the extraordinary powers people have developed. The Church's teachings should lead us in this. She writes:

> In the world's picture ... human beings can more and more be killed so that others can have the life they think they want: human dignity is not a fact to make you behave with reverence before any human life, but rather a standard which it is demanded life should reach ... The Church makes no requirement of a standard before it reverences human life.[7]

We are supposed to revere human life, however young or old, talented or inept, shabby or wicked or foolish or stunted the human beings around us may be. I take it that she would not say that we should do this because of Church teaching. Instead, she would say that Church teaching is as it is because of the sanctity of human life. She writes:

> What people are for is, we believe, like guided missiles, to home in on God, God who is the one truth it is infinitely worth knowing, the possession of which you could never get tired of, like the water which if you have you can never thirst again, because your thirst is slaked forever and always. It's this potentiality, this incredible possibility, of the knowledge of God of such a kind as even to be sharing in his nature, which Christianity holds out to people; and because of this potentiality every life, right up to the last,

---

[7]G. E. M. Anscombe, "On *Humanae Vitae*," in *Faith in a Hard Ground*, p.198. Anscombe was writing about Church teachings on human sexuality specifically, but I take it that the point holds generally for the orientation we seek toward human good and human need and desire.

> must be treated as precious. Its potentialities in all things the world cares about may be slight; but there is always the possibility of what it's for. We can't ever know that the time of possibility of gaining eternal life is over, however old, wretched, 'useless' someone has become.[8]

Suppose We Lack Faith and Hope?

Revealed knowledge about God's acts gives us a strong account of the sanctity of human life and the reverence we owe our fellow human beings as such. Put bluntly, any time a Christian encounters a human being the Christian knows that Christ died for that very human being, and that very human being therefore might enjoy eternal life with God. It is *not* hard to see why one should have reverence for a fellow creature under the circumstances. But suppose we cannot rely on this revealed knowledge of God's acts. Anscombe recognized that it is extremely difficult to give the right sort of account of human good, human psychology, and human life to capture the special reverence we owe human beings without some understanding of the spiritual life of human beings and our relation to divinity.

On some interpretations, however, Aquinas offers part of an account of what can be said on behalf of genuine pursuit of human good without adverting to revelation. I have in mind interpretations of Aquinas's understanding of pagan virtue. Aquinas holds that the inclination to pursue good and avoid evil is operative in every creature. In human beings, this makes itself felt through natural law and natural understanding of human good. Acquired virtues— principally practical wisdom, temperance, courage, and justice—help to orient

---

[8]G. E. M. Anscombe, "Contraception and Chastity," in *Faith in a Hard Ground*, p. 173.

us and foster cooperation among our powers for the sake of reasonable, coordinated pursuit of human good.

Now, fans of Aquinas (and Anscombe clearly was among these) will realize that Aquinas's understanding of the role of virtue in human life and pursuit of human good is significantly indebted to Aristotle. Aristotle counts as a pagan philosopher, of course. And Aristotle's account of virtue raises the possibility that we can account for some sort of coordinated, ordered pursuit of human good without adverting to divinity. Aquinas is perfectly clear that I need no knowledge about God to be alive to and alert to the precepts of natural law. Although this is not enough to establish that we do not need to understand that our final end, by the grace of God, is beatitude in order to have a sound account of acquired virtue, we might make some headway on finding something worth revering in humankind (without reference to spirituality and divinity) by meditating on pagan virtue. In effect, on my reading, this is part of the reason that Anscombe directed our attention to Aristotle in "Modern Moral Philosophy."[9]

Now, there is tremendous controversy among Aquinas scholars concerning whether or not Aquinas believed that pagans could perform genuinely good acts, and whether pagans could acquire genuine virtues (on some readings of Aquinas, those concerns are identical). What Aquinas said was that pagan virtues are in a sense imperfect. I side with the scholars who hold that Aquinas thought that pagans could, nevertheless, acquire genuine virtues. It belongs to this interpretation to hold that pagans could acquire some measure of genuine prudence or practical wisdom, which is the virtue that coordinates and renders reasonable inclinations and passions for the sake of good action. Angela McKay Knobel has made a strong case for such a reading. She writes:

---

[9]G. E. M. Anscombe, "Modern Moral Philosophy," *Philosophy*, Vol. 33, No. 124 (January 1958): 1-19.

> Aquinas believes that original sin does indeed hamper the pagan's ability to acquire the virtues, but that he also believes that it does not prevent him from acquiring genuine virtues that are connected by acquired prudence. To the contrary, the pagan's limitations merely prevent him from possessing virtues ordered to supernatural beatitude and from acting in complete conformity with the natural virtues that he does acquire ...
>
> The acquired virtues order man to the good commensurate to his nature, and prior to the fall—thanks to the gift of original justice—man could have achieved this good. Original sin, however, impedes man's ability to acquire virtue. Original sin does not destroy the principles that order man toward virtue and does not destroy (though it does diminish) man's natural inclination toward virtue, but it does destroy the gift of original justice. Without original justice man's reason no longer has perfect control over the powers of the soul, and reason itself is no longer perfected by God and subject to him. Because of this, the other powers of the soul become disordered. As a result, the pagan can acquire virtues, but the virtues he acquires will only enable him to 'to abstain from evil deeds in most cases, and especially from those which are most contrary to reason.'[10]

On this reading, if we side with Aquinas in holding that human beings are directed to pursue good and avoid bad by nature, that virtues are strengths that help us to actualize the practical direction we have as creatures, and have enough of reason in us to grasp both the sort of direction we are meant to have, and a social world that can help us cultivate the strengths we need to help us in harmonious movement toward human

---

[10]Angela McKay Knobel, "Aquinas and the Pagan Virtues," *International Philosophical Quarterly*, Vol. 51 (2011), p. 342.

good and away from human bad, then pagans can cultivate virtue, but virtue that does not understand its supernatural end. This doesn't alter the teleological force of virtue. It just requires revelation to grasp it. But, then, on my reading of Aquinas (which I take to be in line with Knobel's and think is in keeping with Anscombe's), even human beings who do understand themselves as having both their source and their destination in God will only manage harmonious practical orientations with the help of grace—with divinely infused virtue supporting the operation of acquired virtue.

There is, then, in Aquinas the possibility of pointing to what makes humans good *qua* human, with seeing this as directly tied to rational animal nature, and with acknowledging that we are the animals for whom doing what it belongs to us to do for our own good is a significant struggle. We do not have to accept revealed accounts of the fall from grace to see that the kind of disorder Aquinas charts in fallen human nature accurately captures our condition as we know it. And we should be able to acknowledge that, provided that human moral psychology is directed at reasonable actions, passions, and motives (even if we rarely achieve these), and provided that there are ways of acquiring virtue to help us in achieving this harmony, we have no way of knowing for sure that a nasty sort of person might not one day mend his ways. As a fellow human being, the possibility is there for him. This much, at least, should give us some measure of regard for our fellow human beings.

And of those who are not yet in a position to have ways to mend, or who have become significantly incapacitated through injury or infirmity? We can at least say that, as human beings, they are the sorts of creatures who might meet the challenge of the ethical successfully, if all went well—they are among those animals for whom ethical conduct is possible, however problematic it may be.

In short, I think that we might draw from Aquinas on human nature, natural law, and pagan virtue to begin to have some resources to say why it is that we should have reverence for our fellow human beings even without adverting to theological accounts of our place in creation.

I do not think that this is as strong an account of the reverence we owe each other as the sort a Christian can supply—Anscombe's picture of us as guided missiles homing in on God. I think that "Because Christ died for that very person" is a better way of explaining why we should be mindful of a fellow human being than the kind of answer that can be sketched in terms of the fact that she and I are alike in that we both are members of the species of creature that faces the challenge of the ethical. Anscombe saw us in our proper glory as fellow human beings created by God and, by His grace, seeking union with Him.

4. Dignity's Transformation: Merit, Equality, and Priority of Coherence over Agreement

Bryan C. Pilkington

I. The Forum

At the 2015 Anscombe Forum at Neumann University, I argued that those who wish to employ the concept of dignity as the foundation for our treatment of others (especially in human rights contexts) face a serious challenge in their efforts to garner agreement. Though it is not common to find persons who argue *against* "dignity,"[1] the diversity of accounts offered and of the roles which dignity is asked to play suggests that dignity supporters might in fact not be supporting the same thing. I also argued that the key to offering a coherent account of dignity is making sense of its meritorious and egalitarian elements. These elements appear to be in tension. Briefly, dignity is employed both as the ground of the equal treatment of human beings, but also

[1]For examples of this, see Ruth Macklin. 2003. "Dignity is a useless concept," *British Medical Journal* 327: 1419-1420, a writing about medical ethics; as well as Steven Pinker's "The Stupidity of Dignity," *The New Republic* (28 May 2008).

as a concept that denotes the best human lives. I showed that two of the strongest accounts of dignity to address this tension – Jeremy Waldron's and Gilbert Meilaender's – failed to resolve it in a manner which allows dignity to play this foundational role.[2]

It does not follow from the failure of these accounts to satisfy the two-fold task of coherence and agreement that we should put dignity aside or, as some critics have argued, that dignity is eliminable from our moral and political discourse without serious consequences. A coherent account of dignity, which resolves the tension between merit and equality, has accomplished quite a lot, indeed. Articulating what dignity is, to whom it applies, and what the normative consequences of taking it seriously are is no easy task. Such an account very well might have satisfied its burden of proof; that is, it might be the case it offers the best explanation of our interest in employing dignity and makes more sense, internally and externally, than other explanations. Proceeding in this manner does not prioritize agreement over coherence.

My task in this paper is to carefully examine one of the accounts I discussed at the 2015 Anscombe Forum to see if it can successfully perform the first task.[3]

---

[2]Jeremy Waldron, "Essay: The Dignity of Legislation," *Maryland Law Review* 54 (1995): 633-665; *The Dignity of Legislation* (Cambridge: Cambridge University Press, 1999); "Torture and Positive Law: Jurisprudence for the White House;" "Dignity and Rank," *Archives Européennes de Sociologie* 48 (2007): 201-237; "Dignity, Rank, and Rights: The 2009 Tanner Lectures at UC Berkeley." Gilbert Meilaender, "Human dignity: exploring and explicating the Council's vision," In Adam Schulman (ed.) *Human Dignity and Bioethics: Essays Commissioned by the President's Council on Bioethics*. President's Council on Bioethics (2008). For my examination of these accounts, see "Dignity and the Challenge of Agreement," forthcoming.

[3]I owe a debt of thanks to John Mizzoni, Philip Pegan, Geoffrey Karabin and all of the participants of the 2015 Anscombe Forum for their helpful criticism and supportive comments.

II. Introduction

The concept of dignity is invoked often in human rights discourse and more generally as support for normative claims about how we treat ourselves and how we treat others. Proponents of dignity face the aforementioned challenge of agreement due, in part, to the diversity of accounts of dignity. These accounts rely on different traditions with distinct histories, derive divergent normative implications from reflection on dignity, and are understood (and misunderstood) by critics in different ways. This illustrates that accounts of dignity, similar to other accounts of foundational moral or political concepts, face both internal and external challenges. Thus, a crucial question for the internal coherence of dignity arises: can an account of dignity make sense of dignity's dual role of grounding equal treatment of others, while specifying only certain kinds of lives or activities which are fitting for human beings?

When President Truman was to be honored by the University of Oxford, Elizabeth Anscombe protested:

> For men to choose to kill the innocent as a means to their ends is always murder, and murder is one of the worst of human actions. So the prohibition on deliberately killing prisoners of war or the civilian population is not like the Queensbury Rules: its force does not depend on its promulgation as part of positive law, written down, agreed upon, and adhered to by the parties concerned.[4]

Anscombe's point was that there is something about these persons that demands deeper consideration, and this consideration depends on more than mere agreement. She elaborates through example, writing, "General Eisenhower...

---

[4]This excerpt is from the 1958 pamphlet, "Mr. Truman's Degree," by Elizabeth Anscombe. Text accessed on 19 September 2009 at: <http://www.anthonyflood.com/anscombetrumansdegree.htm>.

is reported to have spoken slightingly once of the notion of chivalry towards prisoners—as if that were based on respect for their virtue or for the nation from which they come, and not on the fact that they are now defenceless."[5] These soldiers are no longer armed and cannot be treated as threats or aggressors. However, there is something deeper than their status as soldiers that requires this respect and which requires a similar respect for noncombatants. With Anscombe's insight in mind, I turn to see if a coherent account of something deeper can be offered.

III. Philosophy, Theology, and Dignity

One of the most contested points in the debate over dignity centers on the concept's connection with religious thought. To merely posit without argument or explanation an account of dignity heavily reliant on religious ideals, practices, or institutions is both philosophically misguided and practically useless. Equally without merit are critiques which reject out-of-hand any account of dignity informed by religious thought. To deny dignity's connection with religious thought is to miss an important part of its history and use. To refuse engagement with the careful and measured work of those informed by religious thought is to miss a worthwhile opportunity to further our understanding of this complicated concept.

The moral theologian Gilbert Meilaender offers an account of dignity from within a theological and philosophical tradition heavily influenced by Christian ideals, practices, and institutions. Through his careful work, the gulf between the meritorious and the egalitarian elements of dignity is illustrated and a possible solution emerges. I argue that this solution maintains coherence in only one instance, when it relies on a claim of theological assertion. Meilaender's other

---

[5] Ibid.

positive arguments fail and his negative arguments prove to be indecisive. The cause of this failure is neither his theological commitments nor the religious context in which he places dignity, as many who have not taken seriously accounts of dignity informed by religious thought might have assumed. Rather, it is Meilaender's inability to relate the two concepts that emerge from his work, which is the cause of this failure. We are left with two distinct concepts of dignity rather than two concepts transforming each other and serving as two elements within one coherent account of dignity, except in the instance of bold theological assertion.

The structure of this paper is as follows. First, I address the two concepts: human dignity and personal dignity. Second, I support the necessity of both concepts in Meilaender's work, and the necessity of each as an element of dignity. Third, I examine the relationship between the two concepts, focusing in particular on the idea of transformation. Finally, I consider three alternative routes to equal personal dignity. One of these routes is best described as a friendly amendment. Two of these routes are clearly rival accounts, but if Meilaender's critiques of these rivals prove decisive, reasons in favor of adopting his account, even in light of the challenge of agreement, are strengthened. I conclude that the friendly amendment is not strong enough to salvage his account and his critiques prove to be indecisive. Thus we are left with two distinct concepts rather than one coherent account of dignity.

Before examining some arguments for the alleviation of the tension between dignity's essential elements, I explain in more detail what the elements are, and why they are essential.

IV. Merit and Equality: Meilaender's Two Dignities

In an essay published in 2008, Meilaender carefully describes the tension between merit and equality as existing between two aspects of dignity, excellence and equality, between an account of dignity that applies to all people to the same degree and an account of dignity that highlights the great achievements of individual human beings.[6] He writes, "Still, I am not persuaded that the Council's discussion is entirely successful, because it seldom does more than set the two concepts of dignity side by side. They do not interact in such a way that the meaning of one can be to some degree reshaped or *transformed* by the other; instead, they remain firmly fixed in separate linguistic compartments."[7] He notes earlier in the same essay, "The general point is, I think, clear, and it seems right to say that, different times and for different purposes, we are likely to speak in either of these ways. Nonetheless, trying to find a way to do justice to each of them simultaneously is no easy task."[8] Taking up this challenge is the task Meilaender performs in his subsequent book, *Neither Beast Nor God: The Dignity of the Human Person.*[9]

Though Meilaender discusses human and personal dignity as aspects of the same concept in his essay, he clearly thinks of them as different concepts in *Neither Beast Nor God*. The differences between these two concepts call for explanation both of their relation to each other and of their mutual operation within a coherent account of dignity.

---

[6]Gilbert Meilaender, "Human dignity: exploring and explicating the Council's vision," In Adam Schulman (ed.) *Human Dignity and Bioethics: Essays Commissioned by the President's Council on Bioethics*. President's Council on Bioethics (2008). Here, he does not argue for two different concepts, but discusses them as different aspects of the same concept.

[7]Meilaender (2008), p. 256, *my emphasis*. Both of these accounts are offered in the President's Council's volume *Human Dignity and Bioethics* (accessible at: https://bioethicsarchive.georgetown.edu/pcbe/reports/human_dignity/) of which Meilaender was a part. The aim of Meilaender's paper in this volume is to explicate different aspects of dignity to which the Council appealed in previous work.

[8]Meilaender (2008), p. 255.

[9]*Neither Beast Nor God: The Dignity of the Human Person*, (Encounter Books, 2009).

Human dignity, as Meilaender uses the term, is a shorthand phrase or a placeholder for a particular vision of human life.[10] As the title of his book aptly suggests, this vision of life focuses on persons as neither beast nor god, but as human beings. It is a vision for a life that is characteristically human and commends engaging in activities and undertaking projects that take seriously our humanity. This is why much of his book is devoted to topics like birth, breeding, childhood, loyalties, and death. Features emblematic of our experience as human must be accounted for when characterizing a full and successful life. This is why human dignity is best thought of as a placeholder for what is characteristically human.

Meilaender's conception of humanity directly informs his account of human dignity. I take this to be the primary reason for his emphasis on anthropology and for the attention he pays to Hans Jonas' philosophical biology.[11] Meilaender writes of anthropology: "I doubt whether we can understand dignity well without at least a modest anthropology – without some notion of what it means to be the sort of creature a human being is. And I, at least, do not think that this understanding can possibly be right if we abstract the human beings we seek to understand from their relation to God."[12]

---

[10]Unless otherwise specified, when I use the phrase "human dignity," I am referring to this notion. If I mean to draw attention to a different account of dignity or a notion of dignity that embodies what Meilaender means by human dignity and by personal dignity, I use "dignity."

[11]Meilaender discusses Jonas' work in his second chapter, "Being Human." Though I do not have space to go into detail on this point, Jonas's focus on metabolism and the purpose of sustaining life should be noted. According to Jonas, human beings are different from other animals in that we do not have what we need to survive. Reflection is important for us. The key point to take away from this for understanding Meilaender's work is the purpose driven, teleological character of Jonas' philosophical biology.

[12]Meilaender (2009), preface. One can see why challenges for agreement looms large.

Human dignity applies to humans. What is worthwhile about noticing this somewhat obvious point is noticing what it does not claim. Those who rely on this point without offering a substantive account of what a human being is cannot rely on the idea of humanity to do any serious work within their account of dignity.[13] And it is worth noting that once such projects have been specified – even if there are many – there will be projects which fail to be characteristically human, pursuits deemed not worthwhile, and, to use Meilaender's phrase, activities that fail to "honor our human dignity." This illustrates that human dignity is a normative concept. Whatever the norms are, there will (almost always) be human beings who fail to measure up. Some will clearly, and I believe uncontroversially, measure lower than others even if they do not wholly fail to pursue what is characteristically human. With a model or a standard for a successful life comes a rubric for measuring lives.[14] Some people will fail to live

[13]An account that focuses on humanity is not barred from extending human dignity to other creatures, for example, an alien that lacked human DNA. This latter point may seem fanciful, but it is worth noting given the surprising number of times it is confused. If we were to come across an alien engaging in projects emblematic of Meilaender's vision of human life, then human dignity is what it would possess – not a related or analogous dignity, but human dignity. Attachments to DNA are puzzling at this point. Recall, that it is an anthropology or a philosophical biology, which is to inform human dignity, not mere biology. I suspect the focus that some place on DNA is meant to head off objections with respect to the equality element of dignity, which we will come to when I address Meilaender's concept of personal dignity.

[14]This rubric need not be very specific and the bar it sets need not be very high. For example, consider a university course in which the assessment of student achievement is based solely on attendance. Whatever the students do – even if they were to sleep through each class – if they showed up to the right room at the right time for the set number of classes, they will receive an A. This measure for the assessment of student achievement is very poor for a number of reasons and we would expect that most students would merit the same grade, an A, regardless of demonstrating competence in the material. This example illustrates a very low bar, but it would be a mistake to assume that all students would merit an A in such a course. Some students will fail to attend the

successful lives. There will be a variety reasons for this failure: ignorance, confusion, and a lack of motivation are just a few. The only way to guarantee that no one will fail would be to have no assessment at all. This is an appropriate segue into the consideration of Meilaender's second concept, for it admits of no measure; everyone succeeds.

In describing personal dignity, Meilaender aims to capture the idea that we are all equal persons whose comparative worth cannot and ought not to be assessed. He writes:

> When we turn to what I have called personal dignity, the notions of comparing or weighing values has no place at all ... But the dignity of the person, which gives each of us equal standing, is not something upon which we can place such a value. The language of personal dignity – because it deals in wrongs, not harms – is used to block these sorts of exchanges. The dignity of each human person is to be respected, which is quite a different thing from being valued.[15]

The concept of personal dignity takes account of the inviolability of all people. The tension between the concept of human dignity and the concept of personal dignity should be clear. Human dignity admits of assessment and gradation. The possession of it can vary from person to person depending upon how each measures up to the standard. Making judgments about different persons and the lives they live is appropriate. Personal dignity is utterly different. All people possess it equally: everyone has it and they have it to the same degree. The personal dignity of a person cannot even be valued; it can only be respected.

---

meetings on time. This will be affirmed by anyone who has taught a university course. The only way to guarantee that no student will fail the course would be to have no assessment at all. Contrast this notion with Meilaender's account of personal dignity where everyone passes the course.

[15]Meilaender (2008), p. 86.

V. The Many Personas of Dignity

To further illustrate the stark difference between personal and human dignity, consider the following four examples.

(i) Jackie Robison

The life of Jackie Robinson is illustrative of the difference between human and personal dignity. Robinson was the first African-American to play Major League Baseball and did so as a member of the Los Angeles Dodgers. He was met with an outpouring of hatred from many who did not even know him. That Robinson played so well amid such treatment is impressive. Describing his conduct and play in any way other than "dignified" seems to fail to capture what we mean when we speak of Robinson. He embodies the excellence and merit associated with high achievement and human dignity. His story is of particular interest because, at the same time, he endured so many violations of his personal dignity. In a statement to his teammates in 1947, Robinson said, "I'm not concerned with your liking or disliking me. All I ask is that you respect me as a human being."[16]

(ii) Betty Purdy

Meilaender's reflection on the character of Betty Purdy illustrates the breadth of the meritorious element of dignity.[17] The relevant passage is the following:

---

[16]Fred Pulis, *The Impact and Legacy Years, 1941, 1947, 1968* (Trafford Publishing, 2000).

[17]Meilaender's 2008 essay was met with the criticism that though he professed to account for both merit and equality, his account of dignity only addressed the former. Diana Schaub argues that in Meilaender's example of Betty Purdy, it is her meritorious character that leads us to affirm her dignity. See Diana Schaub. 2008. "Commentary on Meilaender and Lawler," in *Human Dignity and Bioethics: Essays Commissioned by the President's Council on Bioethics* (Washington, D.C., 2008), pp. 284-293.

> Suppose, however, that our understanding of comparative excellence were reshaped somewhat by a sense of equal human dignity. Then we might speak more as a character named Dinny does, in John Galsworthy's novel *One More River*, when reflecting on the death of old Betty Purdy:
>
> "Death! At its quietest and least harrowing, but yet-death! The old, the universal anodyne; the common lot! In this bed where she had lain nightly for over fifty years under the low sagged ceiling, a great little old lady had passed. Of what was called `birth,' of position, wealth and power, she had none. No plumbing had come her way, no learning and no fashion. She had borne children, nursed, fed and washed them, sewn, cooked and swept, eaten little, travelled not at all in her years, suffered much pain, never known the ease of superfluity; but her back had been straight, her ways straight, her eyes quiet and her manners gentle. If she were not the `great lady,' who was?"

The point here is that who the great human beings are is not obvious. Different realizations of greatness might be associated with human dignity, and even in those who live simply.[18] The final line of the passage illustrates the beginnings of the transformation that must take place between dignity's meritorious and egalitarian elements. This becomes even clearer when we focus on human dignity as a placeholder for what is characteristically human. Betty Purdy shows us that human dignity can be extended to cover many people – not just the Robinsons or Curies or Mozarts.

(iii) Dostoyevsky's Underground Man

At the other end of the spectrum, we might consider the author of Dostoyevsky's *Notes from Underground.* The great

[18]Meilaender (2008), p. 256.

achievements of Robinson and humble virtues of Purdy might both illustrate human dignity. The author of the *Notes* lives a wretched, disgusting life. He begins his *Notes*, writing:

> I AM A SICK MAN.... I am a spiteful man. I am an unattractive man. I believe my liver is diseased. However, I know nothing at all about my disease, and do not know for certain what ails me. I don't consult a doctor for it, and never have, though I have a respect for medicine and doctors. Besides, I am extremely superstitious, sufficiently so to respect medicine, anyway (I am well-educated enough not to be superstitious, but I am superstitious). No, I refuse to consult a doctor from spite. That you probably will not understand. Well, I understand it, though. Of course, I can't explain who it is precisely that I am mortifying in this case by my spite: I am perfectly well aware that I cannot "pay out" the doctors by not consulting them; I know better than anyone that by all this I am only injuring myself and no one else. But still, if I don't consult a doctor it is from spite. My liver is bad, well – let it get worse![19]

This example is worth reflecting on because it illustrates one way in which a person may fail to possess human dignity. We may wonder about the author, as Dmitry did of his father in another of Dostoyevsky's novels, "Why is a man like that alive? ... No, tell me, can he really be permitted to go on defiling the earth with his person?"[20] Meilaender answers "yes." Even though the author lacks human dignity, he retains his personal dignity.

---

[19]Fyodor Dostoyevsky. *Notes from Underground*, trans. Jessie Coulson (London: Penguin Books, 1864), p. 1.

[20]Fyodor Dostoyevsky, *The Brothers Karamazov*, trans. David McDuff (London: Penguin Books, 1880), See p. 100.

(iv) A Case of PVS[21]

It is worth reflecting on those who are considered to be in permanent vegetative states because these cases illustrate another way in which someone may possess personal dignity, but fail to possess human dignity. Unlike the previous example, a person in a permanent vegetative state lacks the ability, possibly through no fault of her own, to engage in a characteristically human life. She still must be treated in the way that personal dignity requires, according to Meilaender.

(v) Four Examples

These four examples illustrate the great difference between personal and human dignity. They are two distinct concepts. One accounts for the equality of all people. The other specifies the kind of life that is best for human beings to live. Given this difference, whether both concepts are necessary and, if so, how they can be simultaneously accounted for become questions of immediate importance.

VI. The Necessity of Both Concepts

Some might argue that dignity's egalitarian element is sufficient to ground human rights claims, noting that values like equality and inviolability, which human rights documents aim to protect, fall within the realm of personal dignity. Though this simpler appeal is tempting, it is problematic for two reasons. First, suppose that there is widespread agreement that personal dignity is sufficient to ground human rights claims. In order to elucidate particular rights from these claims, we must know more about dignity. We must be

[21] The term "PVS" has come under scrutiny because referring to human beings as vegetables is degrading. I use the term only because of its common use and do not mean to degrade or to marginalize those who are considered to be in this state.

able to specify the content of the relevant rights. Reflection on dignity's meritorious element is necessary for this and, in turn, to make a genuine appeal to dignity. Further, any appeal to dignity will, even if not explicitly, involve claims of the form that are associated with Meilaender's human dignity. To say only that human beings are inviolable is not enough. The common but superficial agreement over dignity illustrates this point quite well. That proponents of drastically opposed and even antagonistic views might come together to support dignity illustrates the emptiness of many accounts of dignity. If we rely solely on personal dignity to inform our treatment of others or to ground human rights, we risk being unable to agree on specific articulations of these rights, in addition to our support for them.

"In general, we cannot make sense or achieve sympathetic understanding of appeals to the concept of dignity unless (whatever terminology we choose to use) we distinguish human dignity from personal dignity, for they involve different sorts of claims," writes Meilaender.[22] I have argued that consideration of dignity's meritorious element is necessary for a full and correct understanding of dignity. Without a concept like human dignity, we will not know which rights to safeguard or how, specifically, to treat others. When focusing on personal dignity, we can arrive at the conclusion that we should treat all people equally, but what this means and what specific prohibitions and positive actions this requires remain unspecified.[23] Thus, understanding the relationship between

[22]Meilaender (2009), p. 84.

[23]This is not to say that personal dignity is a purely formal notion; it is not. If a being possesses personal dignity but not human dignity, it still commands treatment akin to that of all other similar beings. My claim is that we will not know what that treatment amounts to and even who the relevant beings are without the further specification that appeals to concepts like human dignity offer.

human and personal dignity is of the utmost importance. Meilaender writes:

> Between the concepts of human dignity and personal dignity there is a dialectical relationship. Each needs the other to supplement its central concern. We need the language of human dignity to talk about matters that involve the integrity and flourishing of the human species, and we need the language of personal dignity to express respect for persons regarded as equal and non-interchangeable individuals.[24]

But we may still wonder why we should not think of these two dignities as completely separate entities, each of which might be employed without the other.[25] What holds them together?

Meilaender argues that it is important to have both concepts in play because each affords protection against the other. The necessary and natural comparisons that arise between persons can lead to an understanding of dignity that focuses only on high achievement. Personal dignity protects against these kinds of comparisons. Similarly, human dignity protects these comparisons, which need to be made in many areas of life, and helps to specify what a flourishing life is for human beings.[26] However, to say that each concept protects against the other is not yet to show that they are both necessary. Further, it does not show how they relate to each other. Is there a priority relationship of some kind and, if so, what kind of priority and which concept takes priority? What is clear is that the protections afforded by including both concepts and the capturing of both the ideals of equality and merit are important for Meilaender's account. He also claims that having both concepts will allow us to see past "surface differences"

---

[24]Meilaender (2009), p. 87.

[25]I argue that we need a concept like human dignity to fill in details regarding our treatment of others, but not that Meilaender's concept is the only option.

[26]Meilaender (2009), pp. 87-88.

between each other and help us to understand those moments of radical equality, such as when our lives are judged "on the whole."[27] This is possible only if we can coherently hold both together, and this is dependent upon Meilaender's account of transformation, to which I now turn.

VII. Transforming Dignities: from Two Concepts to One Account

Thus far, I have stressed the necessity of dignity's meritorious and egalitarian elements, and for Meilaender's account the relationship between human and personal dignity. I offered three reasons for the latter. First, without a successful transformation, we will not have one coherent account of dignity, but rather two independent concepts, which may come apart and be appealed to separately. Second, it is important to understand the history of dignity to try to make sense of both elements of its most important tension and the thought through which this tension has emerged. Finally, there is the practical worry that without this kind of account, we will be unable to employ dignity in a genuine and effective way (that is, the implications of taking dignity seriously for our actions and judgments will be left uninformed to a great degree).

(i) The Transformation

The aim of these arguments is to alleviate the tension within an account of dignity that relies on both the concepts of personal and human dignity. We have seen that if we take both of these concepts seriously they come apart very easily and may even contradict each other. This calls for an explanation of their relationship, which Meilaender gives in

[27] Meilaender (2009), pp. 97.

terms of each concept transforming the other. There are a few possibilities.[28]

One formulation of these kinds of arguments is to identify the two concepts, highlight where they diverge or appear to be inconsistent, and remedy this tension by locating the concepts within a particular context in which both concepts make sense together. There is an ownership claim associated with many of these arguments (and those Meilaender thinks most successful): that these concepts are originally at home within a specifically religious context; and thus, it should be no surprise that this tension arises outside of such a context. Reflecting on dignity from within a different context, one may not have the same resources readily available to alleviate the tension or show that no tension, in fact, exists.

To illustrate how this kind of argument proceeds, consider the three steps of the general argument.

The first step is to identify the two concepts under consideration and highlight the aspects in tension. Meilaender writes:

> Discussing the topic of murder, and replying to an "objection" (as the structure of the Summa calls for such replies), St. Thomas Aquinas writes, "a man who sins deviates from the rational order, and so loses his human dignity [dignitate humana].... To that extent, then, he lapses into the subjection of the beasts....' We may contrast this with the words of Pope John Paul II

[28]It is worth emphasizing that in addition to the mutual protection, two benefits of the transformation are both rooted in personal dignity: seeing past surface differences and considering our lives "on the whole." Additionally, some arguments for this transformation depend on theological claims, others are more generally applicable and might have a greater chance of garnering broad agreement. Though Meilaender allows for a secular route to this transformation, he is not confident that the transformation can be understood apart from situating ourselves within a particular theological context in which both concepts are at home.

> in the encyclical letter Evangelium Vitae, released in 1995: 'Not even a murderer loses his personal dignity [dignitate].'[29]

This paradigmatic example of deviating from the rational order is so antithetical to living a characteristically human life that Aquinas judges the murderer to have lost his human dignity. Yet, according to Pope John Paul II, a person's personal dignity cannot be lost, even in this extreme case. Human dignity can be lost (and, what appears as likely, gained), whereas personal dignity cannot.

In continuing to contrast the two concepts, Meilaender considers three ways in which the President's Council on Bioethics had employed them:

> A distinction between two different senses in which one might speak of human dignity is emphasized in Taking Care. The Council speaks of this distinction in different ways. It notes, for instance, that the language of dignity might be used to mark either a "floor," a kind of respect and care beneath which our treatment of any human being should never fall-or it might be used to mark a "height" of human excellence, those qualities that distinguish some of us from others (106 f.). Similarly, it contrasts a non-comparative manner of speaking about the worthiness of human lives with various kinds of comparative assessments (whether in economic terms or in terms of nobility) of human worth (103 f.). Or yet again, it notes a difference between an "'ethic of equality' (valuing all human beings in light of their common humanity)" and an "'ethic of quality' (valuing life when it embodies certain humanly fitting characteristics or enables certain humanly satisfying experiences)" (106).[30]

[29]Meilaender (2008), p. 253.
[30]Meilaender (2008), p. 255.

We can see the tension taking shape in Meilaender's recounting of the ways in which the Council, of which he was a part, articulated the tension (or "distinction") within dignity. Though there is much here that is clarifying and helpful, not all of it is, and it would be a mistake to take it all on board. Of the three points, the discussion of the tension as marking either a "floor" or a "height" is more misleading than it is illuminating and should be discarded. The metaphors of floor and height suggest a continuum. They invite us to think of dignity as something which admits of degrees and that these degrees can be placed on a scale from the floor to the height. However, the floor, as it is considered here, governs our treatment of others, whereas the height points to the excellent carrying out of those activities that are characteristically human. Even if it were clear that personal dignity relates to treatment and human dignity to qualities, neither the concepts nor what they relate to can be on the same scale, which is even more difficult to make sense of given the Council's treatment of dignity as a single concept. Ignoring these serious issues, imagine we could construct a single dignity scale. There is no good reason to think that there should be a correlation between changes in quality and changes in treatment, which is necessary to make sense of the Council's claims here and the subsequent metaphors.[31]

The other two ways the Council articulates dignity also help to give shape to the tension. The second, which focuses on the differences in acceptability of comparisons ("yes" for human dignity, "no" for personal dignity), and the third, which focuses on characteristically human experiences (connected with human dignity) and equality (connected with personal dignity), are worth reflecting on. However, as I have already

[31] This is part of the ad hoc issue involved in scalar accounts of dignity with a cutoff.

addressed what Meilaender says about these, I shall not do it again.

These three ways of articulating dignity within a bioethical context help to form the background from which Meilaender works. He asserts, "A concept of dignity that emphasizes differences of worth falls harshly on our ears because we have learned to move in the opposite direction"[32] The concept of human dignity appears elitist and aristocratic in a way which clashes with many modern egalitarian intuitions and offends our democratic ideals.[33] (Something, Meilaender argues, personal dignity will protect against.) However, when presented with those among us who courageously stand up to persecution and march toward great accomplishment in a way that is best be described as dignified, to suggest one example of excellent, characteristically human behavior, we may find that we possess contrary intuitions. (Something, Meilaender argues, human dignity will protect against.) For example, recall the description of Robinson's consistent pursuit of athletic excellence in the face of both skilled opponents and bigotry.

I hope that these comments and the earlier comments regarding anthropology and philosophical biology offer enough background material to build up the context from which Meilaender operates.[34] Meilaender's preferred context is explicitly theological, and the practical challenge looms large. The cost of taking on an entire religious framework within a vast and detailed theological context is not cheap. However,

---

[32]Meilaender (2008), p. 261.

[33]Meilaender (2008), p. 260.

[34]An essential feature of this context is its inclusion of religious belief. Meilaender has two compelling arguments rooted in the idea that human beings are equidistant from God. I address these arguments, and show why they fail, elsewhere. (See my "Dignity and the Challenge of Agreement," forthcoming, for these arguments.)

this might be the only viable option for salvaging dignity's meritorious and egalitarian elements.

(ii) Some Transformative Arguments

Meilaender offers a set of arguments for the transformation of human and personal dignity rooted in the idea that human beings are equidistant from God, but as I have shown[35] elsewhere these arguments fail. What is left of Meilaender's positive view is a claim of theological assertion. He notes, "And often, in fact, we do little more than posit an equality about which we are, otherwise, largely mute; for the truth is, as Oliver O'Donovan has assertively put it, that this belief 'is, and can only be, a *theological assertion*.' We are equal to each other, whatever our distinctions in excellence of various sorts, precisely because none of us is the "maker" of another one of us."[36]

Claims of assertion are neither persuasive to those who are not already on board nor are they uncommon in quite sophisticated discussions of dignity. For example, Jeremy Waldron's account of dignity relies on assertion, albeit of a different kind, in attempting to alleviate the tension between dignity's meritorious and egalitarian elements.[37] The problem facing claims of assertion, which I am concerned with in this paper, is not their apparent lack of persuasive force to others. I mentioned the challenge of agreement at the outset, but bracketed this worry with the aim of focusing on the coherence of an account of dignity. Rather, the problem is that this claim of assertion appears to merely avoid the tension, instead of transforming elements of it. However, this need not be a devastating criticism of

---

[35]I argued this position at the 2015 Anscombe Forum, and a version of the argument is forthcoming in "Dignity and the Challenge of Agreement."

[36]Meilaender (2008), pp. 263-4, *my emphasis*.

[37]See my "Dignity and the Challenge of Agreement," forthcoming.

Meilaender's account. If other rival accounts cannot offer better options, that is, if Meilaender's critiques of alternatives are decisive, assertion (theological or otherwise) might be the best option. To examine this possibility, I consider Meilaender's arguments against two rival accounts, and in favor of a friendly amendment.

"When the view that grounds human dignity in our relation to God begins to recede in the minds of some thinkers, the theoretical case for equal respect must be made – if it can be made – on other grounds," writes Meilaender,[38] and with this in mind, I examine his consideration of three attempts to bridge the gap between dignity's meritorious and egalitarian elements that might gain broad appeal.[39] These attempts are better thought of as rival accounts than as opponents of Meilaender's view. Meilaender offers critiques of each, and if these critiques are decisive, we have more reason to side with Meilaender's account even with the challenges it raises for agreement. In what follows, I focus here on alternative routes to equal personal dignity (or support for the egalitarian element of dignity).

(a) The Argument for Equal Personal Dignity from Freedom

Call the first argument the K-view.[40] According to the K-view, the freedom to choose a way of life and to prescribe

---

[38]Meilaender (2009), p. 89.

[39]This should be seen as an exploration into Meilaender's consideration of other possibilities for alleviation of the tension between equal personal dignity and unequal human dignity. As such, I do not try to reconstruct the original arguments of each considered view in their entirety nor offer robust defenses of the positions he rejects. Rather, I consider Meilaender's account of each view in order to better situate his account of dignity and to highlight where specific disagreements arise.

[40]I call this the K-view to avoid interpretative disputes and clarify my focus, Meilaender's account of Kantian freedom. This route to personal dignity is often taken through the notions of equal respect or autonomy. There has been

for ourselves our own norms is the best way to understand personal dignity. Meilaender argues that the K-view runs into three problems. First, it might "lose the body and the human dignity of bodily life."[41] Second, it might lead us to "no longer come to terms with the purposes (or even destiny) built into organic life."[42] Finally, he worries, "No longer simply made in the image of God, [we] are now free spirits, almost godlike [ourselves]."[43] These objections to the K-view's focus on freedom as a route to salvaging personal dignity are similar, but it is worth considering each separately.

First, let us consider the claim that the K-view's emphasis on freedom cannot account for the human dignity of bodily life. It is according to those characteristically human features, which human dignity addresses, that we may excel past others or fall behind them. An emphasis on freedom will not allow for the same characteristic human features as Meilaender does. It will clearly not focus on things such as birth, breeding, childhood and death. But why is this objectionable? We should note that, according to his own account of dignity, a being might not exhibit any of the characteristic human features necessary to merit any level of human dignity and may still possess equal personal dignity. Thus, that the K-view does not take into account characteristically human features that are associated with our bodily existence does not seem necessary for building

---

a great deal of work done on these topics. For example, see Stephen Darwall, *The Second Person Standpoint: Morality, Respect, and Accountability* (Cambridge: The President and Fellows of Harvard College. 2006). For more on this, see two of his papers, as well: Stephen Darwall, "Respect and the Second-Person Standpoint," *Proceedings and Addresses of the American Philosophical Association* (2004) 78.2: 43-59; and Stephen Darwall, "Precis: The Second-Person Standpoint," *Philosophy and Phenomenological Research* (2010) 81.1. See also Ronald Dworkin, *Taking Rights Seriously* (Harvard University Press, 1978).

[41] Meilaender (2009), p. 89.

[42] Ibid.

[43] Ibid.

up an adequate notion of equal personal dignity. Given the K-view's emphasis on freedom and self-prescription of norms, we would not expect it to offer the same account of human dignity that Meilaender does. If this is the measure by which we judge the acceptability of routes to equal personal dignity, then we are not left with much but Meilaender's account.

Alternatively, we might read this criticism as a weaker claim. It may be meant simply to point out that human beings possess bodies and so an account of personal dignity will be inadequate unless it can make sense of this human feature. But notice that the K-view could very well take into account aspects of bodily life relevant for personal dignity. Bodily integrity, for example, would be quite important for sustaining rational thought and for engaging in freely chosen personal projects. Thus the K-view can appeal to the body and, in fact, it seems quite likely that it would. There is a lesson to be drawn from consideration of this problem. If any alternative route to personal dignity must fit perfectly with Meilaender's account of human dignity, we should not expect to find an alternative route. If an allowance is given for some flexibility regarding the details of an alternative account of human dignity, then finding an alternative route to personal dignity is possible.

The next objection to the K-view, like the first, centers on loss: we may lose the teleology built into organic life. Again, I take it that Meilaender is referring to things such as breeding, birth, childhood, and death. Consider breeding. We might, especially after comparison to other animals, see breeding as something that living beings should engage in. It is an end that should be sought, which is built into organic life. However, if such an end is left to our choice, as will be the case with the K-view, the organic purpose is lost.

It seems that a proponent of the K-view should bite the bullet here. The K-view gives weight to rational ends and the capacities or abilities associated with them. Measuring up to certain standards of characteristic human activity falls within the scope of human dignity, not personal dignity. Without repeating the K-view proponent's response to the last objection, I just note that a pattern is developing here. We may also notice that it is not clear whether either side alone bears the burden of proof.

This brings us to the third objection, that we will be godlike ourselves instead of those in-between creatures whose lives Meilaender has so carefully described. Here, again, the proponent of the K-view may register the same response. It becomes clear (if it has not already), with a specific claim about the kind of being under consideration, that we are dealing with different conceptions of the person and, because of this, different accounts of human and personal dignity. Meilaender relies on a conception of the human person, informed by a particular religious context, specifically, by a particular philosophical biology. The K-view is informed by a different conception of the person with a focus on freedom and rationality.

The K-view does not give as much weight to the body as Meilaender does, but it may still be able to offer a compelling case for personal dignity. In noting certain features of Kant's moral theory – a paradigmatic example of the K-view – which have been overlooked, Allen Wood discusses the importance of "Kant's conception of human dignity," defining it as, "the absolute, hence equal, worth of all rational beings."[44] In addressing the oft-mistaken reading of Kant's discussion of duty as it relates to his example of beneficence and the worry that the prototypical Kantian agent performs actions grudgingly and only because of some external constraint, Wood writes:

> What we are told about the motive of duty in Section Two of the *Groundwork* helps further to correct the

[44]Allen W. Wood, *Kant's Ethical Thought* (Cambridge: Cambridge University Press, 1999), see page xiv.

> unappealing conception of this example that Kant's readers often form. For there Kant identifies the "motive" (Bewegungsgrund) proper to morality with the dignity of humanity as an end in itself ... the sorrowful man who acts from duty is not moved simply by the annoying thought "it is my duty to help" but rather acts out of a recognition that those he helps are beings whose worth as ends in themselves gives him a reason to help them. He may not care for them out of sympathy, but he does care for them as beings who have *dignity*.[45]

To repeat, it is not clear that a proponent of the K-view shoulders a greater burden of proof than Meilaender. Adjudication may require engagement between the two theories at a deeper level. This will not be easy as they appeal to different resources and rely on different assumptions. However, as far as an alternative to equal dignity is concerned, the K-view has not yet been decisively knocked down. We are physical beings and that the physical has been relegated is a worthwhile point for reflection. However, more work must be done to show that the K-view cannot meet its burden.

(b) The Argument Against Shared Frailty

Another route to equal personal dignity that Meilaender considers is "roughly Hobbesian." In arguing against it, he also argues against similar rights-based accounts of dignity.

For ease, call these routes and accounts the H-view. Meilaender describes the H-view, writing, "to accent our shared vulnerability, which makes us approximately equal sharers in a life that threatens to be… 'solitary, poor, nasty, brutish, and short.'"[46] However, this emphasis on "shared frailty may create as many problems as it solves," according to

[45]Wood (1999), p. 37.
[46]Meilaender (2009), p. 89.

Meilaender, by "encouraging us to do whatever may be needed to relieve suffering, to sustain and extend life, or just to satisfy our desires, this ground for equal personal dignity is likely ... to undermine important aspects of human dignity."[47]

The proponent of the H-view might offer one of the following two responses to Meilaender's charge. First, she might argue against Meilaender's exploitation of the difference between shared frailty and shared vulnerability. This change in Meilaender's terminology occurs in back-to-back sentences, so it does not seem likely that it is unintended. He refers to accenting our shared vulnerability, moving immediately to describe the shortcomings of a concept of personal dignity based on our shared frailty. This is odd because he argues that we cannot arrive at an adequate account of personal dignity if we root this dignity in our shared frailty; however, we might be able to if we root personal dignity in our shared vulnerability.[48] In describing the recognition of our shared vulnerability, Meilaender discusses the importance of our "common subjection to mortality" and to "death,"[49] but these are clearly things that the H-view can take on board. So what is the difference? Meilaender's objection to the H-view's focus on frailty is that it will lead to the undermining of important aspects of human dignity. Here, the proponent of the H-view may offer the same response that the proponent of the K-view did. If an alternative route to personal dignity requires taking on board Meilaender's account of human dignity in all its detail, no route other than his will satisfy. Proponents of the H-view, like those of the K-view, have their own understanding of human life. However, if they cannot account for important

[47] Ibid.

[48] Meilaender (2009), p. 96. Reflection on the work of Gabriel Marcel is worthwhile here. See especially Gabriel Marcel, *The Existential Background of Human Dignity* (Cambridge: Harvard University Press, 1963).

[49] Meilaender (2009), p. 96.

aspects of our lives, then we should think that they are missing something and this might be a good reason to adopt a context like Meilaender's, even with its cost. Can the H-view respond to this challenge? To explore this possibility, I consider a paradigmatic example of one such aspect of our lives.

In a wonderfully titled section, "Men as Mushrooms," Meilaender argues that we have special relationships, not an uncommon point from someone interested in virtue, which obligate us in particular ways, and that the political lens through which Hobbes considers us is unable to take account of this fact.[50] He claims, "Hobbes's human beings are all will and choice – and no body" and so cannot make sense of relations between the generations.[51] The upshot for the H-view is that it cannot take account of the importance of family in our lives, as it conceives of all relations as essentially political.[52] Consider one example offered in support of these claims. This example is supposed to be illustrative of the inability of the H-view to make sense of important aspects of our lives, aspects that make sense through appeals to dignity. Meilaender writes:

> ... the language of rights cannot account fully for the family's importance in human life. A father's rights have not necessarily been violated if he is unable to feed his children. Nonetheless, his human dignity is diminished. And a decent community will do what it can to avoid this, not because the father has a right to feed his children, but because the human dignity we share is undermined when he cannot.[53]

Meilaender argues that ensuring that a father can feed his children is a mark of a decent community and that this

---

[50]Meilaender (2009), pp. 25-26.

[51]Meilaender (2009), p. 27.

[52]Ibid.

[53]Meilaender (2009), p. 26.

is the case because to fail to do so would allow the father's human dignity to be diminished. Even if the H-view gives us the correct verdict – that a decent community will not allow parents to fail to feed their children – it gets the explanation wrong: this is bad, at least in part, because the father's human dignity is diminished.

Though Meilaender's argument poses a serious challenge, the H-view can better account for this aspect of our lives than he believes it can. A proponent of the H-view may offer the following response:

> *Yes, I construe the problem a bit differently: it is a very bad thing that children are not fed and given the way society is set up, it is the responsibility of parents to feed their children. When a child goes hungry, her rights are violated. It is true that I focus on the child and not the parent, but I can still make sense of something going badly for the parent even if I explain the situation in terms of rights violations.*

We must consider the situation in more detail to see what the H-view lacks. Consider some different instances in which the father's human dignity might be diminished:

> CONTRIBUTION: Suppose the father contributed to a general fund to feed all children of the community or it was understood that his tax dollars went to this effort. His children are his priority and he took steps to ensure they would be fed.
>
> CURLING, NOT FOOD: Suppose the father spends his time and resources on his curling team. He works constantly to improve their strategy and pays for advanced equipment. He has nothing left with which to feed his children.
>
> NO FAULT, NO FOOD: Suppose the father does all he can to provide for his children. However, due to the great

poverty he lives in, he is unable to feed them. He is not responsible for his impoverished situation.

With some details of the example filled in, we can now evaluate what Meilaender and the proponent of the H-view might say about it. In each of these more detailed cases, Meilaender would hold that the father's dignity is diminished. He claims that the father's human dignity is diminished, but as we are searching for a route to equal personal dignity, it is worth considering the possibility he is using "human dignity" loosely here, and really means dignity. If Meilaender means dignity, this would allow personal dignity to do much of the work. Suppose this is the case. If so, the evaluation he would give of CONTRIBUTION might be quite similar to the evaluation of the H-view. The personal dignity of the father, and also the children, is violated. They are not treated as equal members of this decent society. The H-view would employ the language of rights, but it is not clear that there need be a substantial difference, only a linguistic one. In CURLING, NOT FOOD, the children's rights are violated by the father, but his rights are not violated. It does not seem that his personal dignity is diminished by a decent society refusing to feed his children, though this might depend on the details of the case (if others were treated differently in similar cases, then we might say the same thing about his rights). In NO FAULT, NO FOOD, the father's rights might be violated as well as the rights of the children, but we should say the same thing about his personal dignity. The similarity of these responses to these situations coupled with Meilaender's rejection of the H-view recommends against the loose reading.

Evaluating each case in terms of human dignity will give us different results. The father's human dignity is violated in all three cases because he cannot feed his children, which is an obligation he has to them because of their special relationship. Meilaender is correct that the H-view will have a more difficult time explaining this special obligation than he will have. However, appeals to convention or to the fact that the children are products of their parents might be options that the proponent of the H-view would take in trying to elucidate a notion analogous to Meilaender's human dignity. Both of these options face challenges. Rooting familial obligations in convention might not offer a strong enough frame for the picture of the family that Meilaender offers. Treating children as products cannot easily overcome his worry about justice between the generations. However, on this point, the H-view is not without resources. The proponent of the H-view might bite the bullet on convention. One can imagine her pointing out that this is just the way things are and, given this, such obligations are as strong as they could be. If things had been otherwise, so too would the obligations, but why think that this decreases their strength given that things turned out this way? With respect to justice between the generations, the H-view might, relying on a conception of the person different from Meilaender's, focus on, for example, justification to others. A proponent might follow T. M. Scanlon,[54] for example, and aim to act in a way that others could not reasonably reject. If the members of future generations are included in the others to which one wishes to justify oneself, one might have an answer to Meilaender's worry about justice between the generations. There are complicated issues that must be addressed here (and a vast literature devoted to questions about justice between generations), which I do not have the space to attend to, but the H-view has responses available to it.

In discussing Meilaender's account, I have tried to show that the H-view can make sense of this aspect of human life – at least to a certain degree – and the claims of human dignity. However, a proponent of the H-view may not wish to do so.

[54]Scanlon, T.M., *What We Owe to Each Other* (Cambridge: Harvard University Press, 1998).

She might point out that the H-view better represents broadly held intuitions about the three cases, intuitions for which Meilaender's account of dignity tries to account. The proponent of the H-view can say that things go badly for the father in all three cases but that the focus of the H-view is the violation of the children's right to food and that, she might claim, is the more pressing matter. Notice that as long as personal dignity is made to account for these intuitions, the H-view can do so, as well. This is not the case if human dignity is relied upon, but then we may miss something of greater importance.

It appears that Meilaender's criticisms of alternative routes to equal personal dignity are not decisive. Where does this leave us? Were they decisive, we would have a stronger reason in favor of accepting Meilaender's account of dignity, even in light of the challenge of agreement. Unfortunately, they were not decisive. I now turn to a possibly friendly amendment in support of Meilaender's view from the work of Kierkegaard.

(c) Artists and Neighbors

The search for something common in all humanity is a plausible starting point for forging a route to equal dignity, and this is why freedom and shared frailty were worthwhile starting points. Though the details are contested, the motivating idea is worth reflecting on, as there may be some version that unites rather than divides. For example, in discussing the Universal Declaration of Human Rights, Meilaender appeals to Mary Ann Glendon's explanation of how agreement on a universal point was reached from such diverse starting points: "the simple fact of the common humanity" shared by all, which he later refers to as our "shared humanity."[55] This kind of recognition may prove to be a useful route to equal personal dignity. As I noted previously, Meilaender is not optimistic

[55] Meilaender (2009), p. 91.

that we can do this outside of a theological context. He says of Glendon's point that her appeal to our common humanity "as morally significant may be nourished by background beliefs whose roots are religious. Indeed, it may be that such an epistemologically particular starting point gives the surest ground for a confidence in ontologically universal claims about the dignity of every human being."[56] However, he does suggest some options, one of which I consider in what follows.

The route to equal dignity that I examine in this section is rooted more deeply in experience than the previous two. This phenomenological focus might fare better than the more theoretical earlier attempts. It should also be noted that the philosopher Meilaender engages here is a religious believer. However the particular account, as I construe it, need not rely on theological claims (or at least, it might not). Meilaender is more amenable to this route, in which he borrows extensively from the work of Søren Kierkegaard.

In this phenomenological route, Meilaender relies heavily on two images from Kierkegaard. The first is the contrasting images of two different artists.[57] The second is the image of the neighbor.[58] I examine each in turn, and do so briefly, as I anticipate that these images will be familiar to most readers. The first artist travels the world, but finds no perfect face to paint. The second artist stays at home professing not to be an artist and unable to find any face so insignificant that beauty cannot be found in it. Kierkegaard's, and Meilaender's, point is that the second of the two painters is the real artist. This is a wonderful image and the point of the contrast – finding worthwhile things in those around us, instead of searching for what might superficially seem more important – is equally nice, but how does this help us arrive at a realization of the

[56] Ibid.

[57] Meilaender (2009), pp. 95-97.

[58] Meilaender (2009), p. 98. He also discusses this in Meilaender (2008).

equal personal dignity of all? There are at least two plausible interpretations of this image. First, the lesson to be drawn from this illustration might be that the first artist has in mind the perfect exemplar of human dignity, which cannot be found, but that lesser reflections of human dignity can be found. But this misses the point. The most pressing worry is not with those who might possess human dignity to a lesser degree than others, but with those who do not possess it at all. Thus, the image needs to contrast something like a third artist who paints faces that are not there or that are so radically deformed as to not be considered faces at all. Second, the lesson to be drawn might be that the first artist only perceives human dignity, missing personal dignity, whereas the second is able to perceive and understand personal dignity's importance. The latter recognizes those beings with personal dignity and affords to them the same status and treats them in the same ways as she would the exemplary subject that the first artist never found. Though this reading does not miss the point of focus, equal personal dignity, its contrast with the other artist highlights the differences in experience and recognition of others as something relevantly similar to us.[59] How, given the

[59]Two additional points might be worth consideration, though I do not take the failure of any of these arguments to undermine the claims of this section. First, Kierkegaard's second artist brings a "certain something with him." (See Soren Kierkegaard, *Works of Love* (Princeton: Princeton University Press, 1847), pp.157-159. If it is something outside of experience then this illustration is not enough to ground equal personal dignity solely on the basis of experience. Also, Kierkegaard's employment of religious sources here shows that what the artist brings in (see his use of the Apostle John throughout this section) is a fully informed religious context. This coupled with the language of duty that Kierkegaard uses later in the section from which the image comes ("Our Duty to Love the People We See") illustrates a striving by the second artist to find something that may not appear without such striving. This further illustrates a reliance on context. Kierkegaard has in mind something religious as that "certain something," but I have put this to the side to see if it is possible to use the resources from this work to arrive at a non-religious route to equal personal dignity. However, this may not be possible via these resources. Second, the

diversity of experiences of dignity (ours and those of others) can we determine which is the true artist?

The second image, Kierkegaard's image of the neighbor, illustrates a kind of love that is applicable to all people, and so is quite fitting for assisting with our understanding of equal personal dignity. The relevant passage from Kierkegaard, to which Meilaender points his readers, is: "There is not a single person in the whole world who is as surely recognizable as the neighbor. You can never confuse him with anyone else, since the neighbor, to be sure, is all people…If you save a person's life in the dark, thinking that it is your friend – but it was the neighbor – this is no mistake."[60] The point of the image and its amenability to equal personal dignity should be obvious. As neighbor is a status held by all people, the treatment due to the neighbor is treatment that is appropriate for all people. However, where this illustration falls short is at exactly the point in the argument where it needs to be the strongest. Equal treatment of all those that qualify as a neighbor is not problematic, but the recognition of other beings as the neighbor is. The neighbor is supposed to be the easiest person to recognize because everyone is the neighbor. However, this is the very point at issue. Given the varying experiences that people have and their differing intuitions regarding those beings that are relevantly "like us," claiming that the neighbor is most easily recognizable and cannot be confused raises a dilemma. Common examples and treatment

---

image's focus on art may help lead to the conclusion inappropriately. We may agree that the real artist is the second artist, but we might do so for a number of reasons: we like to see flawed examples painted, we think the artist rose to a challenge, or we have an aesthetic appreciation of the work's technical rigor utterly devoid of its subject. (We might enjoy paintings of murder or accounting but not think that there is anything worthwhile in the activities painted and even think that the former is abhorrent.) These might be reasons to favor the second artist as the real artist, but none of them leads us to a realization about equal personal dignity.

[60]Meilaender (2009), p. 98.

of others illustrate that people do not always (or even often) recognize others – their neighbors – as like them. This suggests that either the neighbor is not as easily recognizable as Kierkegaard and Meilaender think, which in turn suggests that experience is not enough to ground dignity; or, the neighbor is easily recognizable, but many people are unable to recognize her or do not realize what they have recognized, which requires some additional standard to determine who counts as a neighbor and who does not. Thus, relying on experience, at least in this manner, is not enough to ground dignity, and so, this phenomenological route to equal dignity appears to fail.

VIII. Conclusion

In this paper, I have examined Gilbert Meilaender's commendable work on dignity. His work takes seriously the tension between dignity's meritorious and egalitarian elements. He argues that human dignity and personal dignity (and thus merit and equality) are not in tension when they are viewed within a particular religious context in which dignity is at home. I have argued that his arguments for a route to equal dignity leave personal and human dignity in tension, except in the case of theological assertion. In the case of theological assertion, it seems more apt to choose a term other than transformation, as the concepts do not really transform each other, but rather seem to suggest different sets of requirements on the lives of persons. One requires treatment of all people to be equal treatment. The other specifies the kind of life that is best to live. Theological assertion in support of the elements of dignity within a particular religious context is enough to offer a picture of dignified human life and connect this with all human beings. However, theological assertion is neither the most persuasive kind of argument nor the kind of argument that can be appealed to when attempting to ground the treatment of others in cooperation with those who do not share this context. It is not the most persuasive kind of argument because it does not yet show how a transformation between dignity's elements occurs.

Part 3

Dignity and Applied Ethics

5. Death and Dignity

David B. Hershenov

Introduction

Ronald Dworkin and David Velleman attempt to justify euthanasia and physician-assisted suicide by appealing to considerations of patient dignity. Dworkin insists that respecting dignity involves acknowledging patients' earlier autonomously produced interests that are retained even when unrecognized by those suffering dementia.[1] Velleman argues for a similar lethal result on the grounds that mind destroying injuries and diseases degrade patients as they undermine their rationality-based dignity.[2] I argue that not only do their projects fail internally for the dignity and interests that they are trying to protect can't do the lethal work they want them to do, but their conceptions of dignity aren't even able to provide

[1]Dworkin, Ronald, *Life's Dominion: An Argument about Abortion, Euthanasia and Individual Freedom* (Knopf, 1993).

[2]Velleman, David, "*A Right of Self-Termination?*" *Ethics* 109 (1999): 606-628.

reasons to cure the extremely demented who are reduced to childlike or comatose states.

The problem for Velleman's account is that a mentally debilitating disease has reduced the patient's rationality-based value to the point that it doesn't make sense to claim he possesses a value that is being continuously degraded in a manner that can be halted only by hastening his death. Moreover, Velleman's insistence that an individual's interests only matter if their possessor is valuable, means that the loss of rationality-based value removes any weighty reason why the diseased individual's destroyed rationality should be restored if it could be. Dworkin's theory fails to realize that the earlier autonomously produced interests in leading a certain life that allegedly require an early death after dementia strikes do not actually survive the brain destruction wrought by Alzheimer's or other mind destroying pathologies. Dworkin's impoverished account of interests, which recognizes only "critical interests" that were autonomously generated prior to the disease or "experiential interests" subsequently manifested by the demented, provides no basis for an interest in a cure that is there in the absence of autonomous capabilities or a conscious wish to be restored to health.

A more promising approach is to recognize that we have welfare interests based on the kind of being we are. There is a certain healthy development and functioning that is proper for us. That life involves the exercise of rational and affective capacities no other known living creatures possess. They bestow upon us a value that isn't shared by any other creatures, even if those creatures are intrinsically no different from our mindless and minimally minded young or brain-damaged adolescents and adults. Due to the fact that we are instances of a kind of entity that can lose out on lives of great value, death harms us to a degree that it does not harm any other kind of living organism. Given the great heights of the benefits and the extreme depths of the losses that creatures of our kind can undergo, our moral status is much greater than that of any other living being. This is true even if the loss is either overdetermined by dementia and death or the loss that death would have brought is preempted by dementia.

My contention is that even our mindless conspecifics have an interest in healthy development. That interest always exists, as health is a necessary condition for flourishing. It explains why our death is a great harm and why we would be harmed if not cured of our dementia. Accounts that find our dignity in our autonomous personhood (Velleman) or earlier capacities to autonomously generate interests (Dworkin) can't account for the moral status and treatment intuitively owed those who never were or are no longer rational persons or consciously interested in their dignity. They can't explain why if there was a scarce serum that could either transform brain-damaged adults into persons or bestow personhood upon healthy kittens, the serum goes to the former.

Part I

Velleman's Account of a Person's Dignity, Good, and Interests

Velleman contrasts the person's value with the person's good or well-being. It makes sense to care about the good of a person only if one values that person. So it is reasonable that a person should care about his own good only if he cares about his value as a person. Velleman illustrates this point with a story about someone who after doing something horrible, loathes himself for he thinks himself worthless (610). As a result, he ceases to care about his good. He can realize that certain things are in his interest, but since he doesn't value himself, he doesn't value his interests. So if a person does not matter, then his interests and his good don't matter (611).

The notion of intrinsic value is at the basis of Kant's moral theory and crucial to Velleman's account. As readers know, Kant calls this value "dignity" and argues that morality requires that we respect people's dignity. We possess dignity because we possess the property of humanity. Kant insisted that morality isn't possible without a belief in the dignity of the person. If a person doesn't have value, nor do his good and interests. Velleman believes that this might sound like the religious notion of the sanctity of life but what he wants is a secular substitute for the sanctity of life. He finds it in our humanity or personhood, i.e., our rational moral agency. This is the foundation for morality. It is this intrinsic value or dignity that morality will honor and protect.

Velleman emphasizes that respect for people's intrinsic value is not the same as respect for human beings. Being a rational person involves having a mind of a certain sort and some human beings don't possess those traits. A mindless fetus is not a rationality possessing person so respect for persons doesn't render abortion immoral. Thus Velleman insists that respect for the intrinsic value of persons doesn't mean such respect is owed to all human life. Dignity is what Kant calls a "self-existent value," one we don't have to bring into existence but must respect when it does exist. Velleman would surely endorse Kant's statement that "In and for itself, life is in no way to be highly prized, and I should seek to preserve my own life only insofar as I am worthy to survive."[3]

According to Velleman, what is missing in debates about physician-assisted suicide and euthanasia is an appreciation of the distinction between our interests and our value. Each of us possesses a value that is greater than ourselves. It is a value that we must live up to even when doing so is not in our interests. Velleman believes that the question people should be asking is "Are we doing justice to our life?" rather than "are we getting enough out of it?" Our dignity puts limits on what we can do in the pursuit of our interests. It imposes restrictions

[3]Kant, *Lecture on Ethics.*

both on what we can do to others as well as what we can do to ourselves. We can act immorally towards ourselves.

However, Velleman doesn't deny that there are situations where someone should be helped to die. Velleman just objects to a person doing a cost/benefit analysis and declaring it is in his interest to die. Velleman insists that it is a form of practical irrationality to pursue what is derivative in a way that destroys or frustrates the very end it serves and that ultimately gives it value. As noted earlier, your interests, well-being and happiness matter because you matter. They are, in a sense, means to the end of respecting your value. They are of derivative value while your rationality and personhood are of non-derivative value. Your dignity is a value *in you* not *for you*. Your dignity is not something valuable because you care about or desire it, you can only respect it or disrespect it.

Since one's interests have derivative value, they cannot be appealed to in order to deny or destroy the non-derivative value that is the very source of their conditional value. Demanding a right to die on the basis that it is in one's interest would be no more coherent than the Catholic Church or another religion establishing an ecclesiastical court and then this court trying to disband or undermine the church (or religion). The court's authority is derived from the church's. So it doesn't have the authority to abolish the church which is the very source of its authority. Replace the authority of the church and court with the value of the person and their interests, and you have the parallel incoherence of an interest-based right to die.

We can also see this incoherence if we assume a patient claiming that his life had little or no value remaining. If he then requests or demands our help to die on the grounds that death is in his interest, why should we help him fulfill the interests of his value-less or nearly worthless life? His interests would be no more valuable than those of furry or winged creatures dying every night in the woods. But if the patient does have considerable intrinsic value, why then should we respect his interest in destroying the source of the value of that very interest? So the derivative value of his interests can't be the ground for destroying the source of their value.

Velleman's Defense of Kantian Suicide for the Sake of our Dignity

Velleman insists that respect for a person's dignity doesn't rule out physician-assisted suicide and euthanasia. It just excludes certain arguments in favor of hastening death. It rejects trade-offs of one's dignity for pain relief. It prohibits what he calls "escapist suicide," where one dies to escape the burdens or frustrations or tedium of life. But if one can no longer live with dignity, then the death of such a person would not offend against his value. It wouldn't involve weighing his interests against his value. If a patient's value or dignity is deteriorating, then out of respect for it, death may be warranted.

Velleman points out that we often destroy objects of value or dignity when their value is under attack. Flags and books are destroyed or buried rather than allowed to continue to deteriorate. Honor guards have a ceremony for removing and destroying tattered flags. They don't leave the flag up until it is fully shredded. Likewise for books: religious Jews bury bibles that are falling apart. Velleman doesn't believe these things have *intrinsic* dignity like persons. But they all belong to the "class of dignity values, whose defining characteristic is that they call for reverence or respect" (617). The dignity of books or flags he claims is borrowed from the dignity of persons. I take that to mean the flag stands for the persons of the countries and their values and the books are an achievement of persons who wrote them and perhaps whose lives they describe.

Velleman writes that "dignity can require not only the preservation of what possesses it, but also the destruction of what is losing it, if this destruction is irretrievable" (617). He stresses that patients should die for the sake of their dignity, not because it is in their interest to be relieved of pain. Velleman points out that there is a difference between pain and suffering. Some people bear their pain well. Others disintegrate in the face of pain. The distress of disintegrating as a person is what Velleman means by "suffering" and that, not pain, "necessarily touches one's dignity" (626). Individuals are not rational selves anymore when they suffer greatly for they can no longer engage in rational activity. They have lost and are losing value, so death to prevent this is not an offense against their value. The suffering may be due to unbearable pain as when one is distressed that most of one's life has become restricted to a focus on pain relief (618). But one can also suffer without physical pain. Someone with dementia may be suffering for they can't be rational agents anymore, or to the degree that they want. They no longer can reason well, recall things, and carry out their plans.

Velleman believes that a person's decision to die would be premature if he possessed all his rationality and just wanted to avoid a future in which it would decline. If one was fully rational, it would be an offense to one's dignity to hasten death. It is only when the dignity is under attack by the disease that death is not an affront to one's dignity. Velleman describes patients in the earlier stages of dementia as being in the "twilight of autonomy." Velleman speaks of the person then as being not fully a person but a person to a lesser degree. Such a "temporally scattered person" will have moments of lucidity followed by confusion. So paradoxically, when the person is rational, she doesn't have a reason to die, but when she has a reason to die she is no longer competent enough to fully recognize and appreciate it. So her choosing death wouldn't be autonomous or fully voluntary. She needs to be involved in the decision but her "self-determination is more of a shadowy presumption than a clear fact" (619).

Only the Dignified can be Degraded

I turn now to criticisms of Velleman's Kantian approach. Insults to dignity in the case of the tattered flag involve the coexistence of the value and the slight. The people that the tattered flag stands for or the values they hold dear coexist with the offensive and degrading treatment. The books that are burned or buried rather than allowed to disintegrate further co-exist with the divine author or the people the story is about or the values they represent. Slavery, perhaps the paradigm case of degrading the dignified, involves people being demeaned while they possess a great unappreciated value. Likewise, to degrade yourself is to act in a way not befitting your value. Value and the offense to it must co-exist. But this temporal co-existence isn't the case for the advanced Alzheimer's patient. So how is the survival of the Alzheimer's patient degrading if his value is gone or nearly gone? He used to be rational, he is no longer - or he is much less rational than he was. Thus if the disease has eroded the rationality and dignity of the patient then its persistence and effects cannot be an offense to the patient's value for that value is gone. At best, the injury or disease can be said to "attack" one's value at the outset but it soon removes one's value and thus is not an offense against any present value. Once someone's cognitive capacities have been undermined, there would be little or no Kantian value to be further offended unlike the case of the ongoing degradation of a rational human being who is enslaved and being treated like a farm animal.

Perhaps the degradation that Velleman has in mind is the suffering of persons earlier in the disease who are still sufficiently aware of themselves and distressed that they cannot act rationally. They retain some value in the Kantian sense for they are not devoid of rationality, and their remaining dignity enables them to feel distress when they are frustrated in their attempts to navigate their world. But I worry that the frustration is not really an offense to their value since a considerable portion of it is gone and the patients are acting as someone with that level of reason should act. If they were undignified, so would be the retarded who are distressed when their cognitive limitations frustrate them. We don't consider the retarded, animals and children to be undignified when they act in a way that is to be expected and appropriate for them given their developmental stage or cognitive inability to do otherwise. We do find undignified those adults who misbehave and act like children when they are capable of acting otherwise.[4] But the demented could not act otherwise and so their behavior is not undignified.

Velleman's idea might instead be that the dignity attack consists of the patient being distressed by the prospect of the disease *further* eroding her value. She realizes she soon won't even be able to do what she now can do. The retarded, animals and children are not facing the same decline. So it may be the awareness that more value will be lost that distresses the person and justifies our assisting them in dying. However, recall that Velleman thought that the killing of the rational before they lost their rationality would be to offend their value. It would be wrong even if they were *very distressed* by the prospect of their entering the twilight of autonomy. So to kill those losing value in order that they will not suffer distress from the prospect of losing more value seems to be liable to the same charge that it is too early if there exists enough value to motivate concern about one's future. Furthermore, if Velleman's idea is instead that after the onslaught of the disease that there is less dignity to offend by appealing to one's interests to die (622 nt. 17), the earlier incoherence threatens to return. Given his account of interests being of derivative value, it seems that even a decline in the value of the demented would mean that

---

[4]See my "Death, Dignity and Degradation," *Public Affairs Quarterly*, 21:1 (2007), 21-36 for some distinctions in usage between *undignified* and *not dignified*.

their non-derivative value (the residual rationality) was being sacrificed for the derivative (an interest in dying).

Velleman can't mean that the offense is to the way the person *ought* to be. That would make it undignified and an offense to be retarded. Surely, Velleman wouldn't think that the distress of the retarded is a reason to hasten their deaths. We typically want the undignified to realize that their behavior is shameful. But we would not want the retarded or the demented to be ashamed and believe it was a mistake to remain alive.[5] Yet Velleman's account suggests that at least the demented are making a mistake clinging to life and should be ashamed of that.

An alternative interpretation is that Velleman believes the patient ought to die because his condition is an offense to the way he *used* to be. That would spare the retarded but provide a reason for others to die even when comatose for they are shadows of their earlier selves. But Velleman seems to indicate that there isn't a dignity-based reason in terminating the irreversibly comatose. He writes "The view stated in this essay is that assistance in dying is morally justified to spare the patient from degradation. This view could hardly justify withholding such assistance until there was nothing left to degrade" (626). However, Velleman does suggest a thing can be an offense to its past when he writes that "the moral obligation to bury or burn a corpse, for example, is an obligation not to let it become an affront to what it once was" (617). But Aquinas and many others argue that the deceased human being doesn't persist as a corpse so *he* can't then be in a state that is an offense to his earlier exalted condition.[6] A

---

[5]See my "Death, Dignity and Degradation," *Op. cit.* for a "shame test" for undignified.

[6]See my "Organisms and their Bodies," *Mind.* 118:70. (2009) 803-809 and "Do Dead Bodies Pose a Problem for the Biological Account of Identity?" *Mind*, 114:453. (2005) 31-59.

corpse is not a dead man but merely his remains. These may warrant a certain respectful treatment but that is because they are *human* remains rather than implicate anything about the dignity of the deceased.

Nevertheless, while the idea of an offense to the way one used to be doesn't apply to corpses for metaphysical reasons, Velleman could extend the idea to comatose or childlike patients, arguing those conditions are an offense to the way they were. But since the two states don't temporally co-exist like the slave and his degrading treatment, this is a very different type of dignity attack. I suspect it is being confused with patients wanting to be remembered at their best. If a patient requesting his own death so others wouldn't see him in such a state would not want to die if he would be unseen by those whom knew him prior to the coma or dementia, then considerations of dignity are not in play. His rationality-based dignity is just as far beneath what it was whether he's seen or unseen. Being remembered at one's best is like wanting to be photographed in a way that is flattering, neither invokes considerations of Kantian dignity.

Therefore it isn't clear to me that Velleman's framework can justify hastening death. But I think Velleman should worry even more that his account can't justify healing the extremely demented or comatose. Imagine that someone has been reduced to infancy or unconsciousness by their Alzheimer's disease. Why cure them by restoring their capacity for rationality, assuming we could? Although we don't presently have the means, imagining a future where we can reveals why the Kantian moral account of our dignity lying in our rationality is insufficient. Recall that Velleman had emphasized that respect for the dignity of persons is not the same as respect for human beings. Being a person involves having a mind of a certain sort and some human beings don't possess these traits. A mindless fetus is not a person so respect for persons doesn't mean abortion is immoral. Velleman went out of his way to note that dignity is what Kant calls a "self-existent value," one we don't have to bring into existence but must respect when it does exist. But how is the comatose or infant-like human adult different from the fetus in a morally significant way? True, the patient once was rational. But why should that matter when there is no remaining physical realization of that intrinsic value? Moreover, recall the earlier Velleman quote that the way one *was* gives us no reason to euthanize the comatose for there is no longer any value that is left to be degraded. So I don't see why we would have any reason in Velleman's framework to help the extremely demented or comatose. It can't lie in their *potential* for rationality for that is there in the fetus that Velleman claims lacks dignity. So the extremely demented either lack an interest in a cure or it doesn't matter very much given their greatly diminished value.

Part II

Dworkin's "Life Past Reason"

We have seen that the decision to die made during the "twilight of autonomy" will not be a fully autonomous decision as it isn't authorized by someone who is determinately a person. That means that such cases of euthanasia will begin to resemble non-voluntary euthanasia. But a possible difference between the euthanasia that Velleman advocates and non-voluntary euthanasia is that the patient could have made an advanced directive when competent and autonomous about how she would want to be treated within the twilight of autonomy. A natural suggestion is that an advanced directive could turn such deaths into voluntary euthanasia since there earlier was a recognition and endorsement of such reasons being applicable later. Dworkin offers such an account.

Dworkin's concern in the last two chapters of his book *Life's Dominion* is with the exercise of antecedent autonomy and the best interests of the severely demented. Dworkin concentrates upon what moral rights people in the late stages of dementia have and what is best for them. He discusses Andrew Firlik's famous account of Margo. Firlik met Margo while doing a medical school gerontology elective. She painted the same circles within circles every day, read randomly the same mystery novel, enjoyed peanut butter and jelly sandwiches, and the company of familiar people whose names she did not know. Firlik memorably described her "as one of the happiest people I know."

Dworkin states that those who were not always demented but became so can be thought of in two ways: a demented person, emphasizing their present situation and capacities; or as a person who has become demented, having an eye to the course of his whole life. Would a competent Margo - before the onset of dementia - have a right to dictate that later life-sustaining treatment be denied, even if, when demented, she pleads for it? It would obviously be incredibly difficult for a doctor to end the life of someone at a time when they presently don't want to die and seem to have no recognition of or interest in their earlier reasons to die – a disdain of a life without intellectual pursuits, a loathing of being dependent and a burden upon others, an inability to recognize loved ones, wanting to be remembered by friends and family in a certain way and so on. It might be thought to help if the doctor imagines the patient briefly regaining lucidity and complaining that her earlier wishes to die were ignored. Then if she lapsed back into dementia, this would elicit the belief that the doctor should heed a person's autonomous wishes not their demented wishes. But this approach is very flawed. It involves the doctor imagining that the patient has interests that she doesn't actually have. I'll come back to this crucial point later.

Dignity, Rights and Dementia

Dworkin observes that a person's dignity is normally connected to his capacity for self-respect (291). Dworkin asks, should we care about the dignity of a demented person if he has no sense of it? He suggests that it "depends upon whether his past dignity, as a competent person, is in some way still implicated. If it is, we may take his former capacity for self-respect as requiring that he be treated with dignity now, dignity is now necessary to show respect for his life as a whole" (220-221).

Dworkin claims that the value of autonomy derives from the capacity it protects, the capacity to express one's own character – values, commitments, *critical* as well as *experiential* interests. Experiential interests are those that please us. Dworkin offers the following description:

> We all do things because, we like the experience of doing them: playing football, perhaps, or cooking and eating well, or watching football, or seeing Casablanca for the twelfth time, or walking in the woods in October, or listening to The Marriage of Figaro, or sailing fast just off the wind, or just working hard at something. Pleasures like these are essential to a good life – a life with nothing that is marvelous only because of how it feels, would be not pure but preposterous. (201)

Dworkin contrasts experiential interests with people's critical interests. He finds critical interests in some ways to be more important than experiential ones. He describes the former as the hopes and aims that lend genuine meaning and coherence to our lives. They express one's considered values, life story and commitments. Critical interests lead people to "want to make something, or contribute to something, or help someone, or become closer to more people, not just because these would be missed opportunities for more pleasure, but because they are important to themselves" (202). Dworkin writes of his own critical interests: "I feel that it is important that I have a close relationship with my children ... that I manage some success in my work ... that I secure some grasp, even if only desperately minimal, of the state of advanced science of my era" (202).

Dworkin believes that respect for autonomy means we must carry out someone's advanced directive or honor antecedent intentions that they made on the basis of their critical interests. Respecting autonomy protects a person's judgment about the overall shape of the life he wants to live. It allows people to live their own lives rather than be led along by their circumstances. Recognizing an individual's right to autonomy makes self-creation possible, so each of us can be what we have made of ourselves. We even allow someone to choose death over amputation or blood transfusion, if that is his informed wish, because we acknowledge "his right to a life structured by his own values... Autonomy encourages and protects people's general *capacity* to lead their lives out of a distinctive sense of their own character, a sense of what is important to and for them" (224). One principal value of that capacity is realized when people live a life that displays a general, overall integrity. Dworkin observes that "Integrity is closely connected to dignity. Moreover: we think that someone who acts out of character...shows insufficient respect for himself" (205).

Precedent Autonomy

Dworkin understands precedent autonomy as a version of integrity-based autonomy. To see how integrity-based precedent autonomy operates, imagine that the incompetent patient earlier executed a living will providing for what he clearly doesn't want now in his debilitated state. Suppose that Margo left instructions to give all her property to charity so it couldn't be spent on her care or that she requested no treatment for any life threatening disease she might contract. Or imagine that she requested to be killed as soon as possible once dementia manifests to a certain degree. Wouldn't respecting autonomy then require her autonomous wishes be carried out despite the pleasure she got from various activities like drawing, eating peanut and butter and jelly sandwiches, and reading her dog-eared mystery novel?

The integrity view supports the view that past wishes must be respected. Advanced directives can be understood as judgments about the overall shape of the kind of life one wants to have led. Someone may object and instead claim that autonomy is necessarily contemporary, i.e., only present decisions, not past ones relinquished, should be respected. Dworkin says that's fine for the competent. But imagine a Jehovah's Witness who demands no blood transfusions, for that will cut him off from God for all eternity. Suppose the accident that created the need for blood also deranged him and he pleads to be transfused. The doctor agrees to transfuse him. Then when the Jehovah's Witness becomes lucid, he is outraged and insists that his autonomous wish was disregarded. Dworkin agrees with his charge. His former decision remains in force because no new decision by a person capable of autonomy has renounced it. It is not because the Jehovah's Witness will later regret his choice to transfuse. If the Jehovah's Witness was competent at the time and in a moment of cowardice, demanded the transfusion, he might certainly later regret it. But the difference is that is a change of mind of the competent. He was competent, however weak, at the time of the change of mind. Respecting his autonomy demands this change be respected.

Dworkin says that if we respect the wishes of the patient in a persistent vegetative state, and courts have ruled that states must, then we have the same reasons not to keep alive those who dread dementia rather than unconsciousness. Dworkin admits that there are troubling consequences. Could we deprive of life, even kill, a rather content Margo? He admits that there might be reasons not to. But he insists that they still would violate her (precedent) autonomy.

Objections to Dworkin's Accounts of Critical Interests

My contention is that most of the critical interests of persons don't survive their dementia. Consider an updating of Parfit's Combined Spectrum thought experiment. A brilliant evil neuroscientist has rewired your colleague's brain, arranging his neurons in the way that Michael Jackson's were arranged. Your colleague no longer has interests in, say, philosophy, classical music and waltzing but now shares the musical tastes of the King of Pop and likes to break dance. Your rewired colleague no longer wants to live in a college town but yearns to move to Jackson's *Neverland* ranch. The neurological structures that have been destroyed were the physiological basis for many of his critical interests. Those earlier critical interests that were contingently acquired and idiosyncratic to your colleague don't remain. Dementia is equivalent to the evil scientist "unravelling" your colleague's neurological connections but not "rewiring" them in the manner of Michael Jackson. The interest in, say, doing philosophy or composing music or living an independent life are destroyed by the disease.

Since the demented have had their earlier interests removed, I don't think there are any antecedently autonomously generated interests remaining to be respected. It is not just that the demented can't recognize and act in accordance with their critical interests, but they don't have them anymore. They are not like the above Jehovah's Witness or you when asleep and still retaining interests of which you are not aware at that time. You can wake and live in accordance with those interests. Your interests are still realized or supported by your brain in some sense. How your brain does this is barely understood but most of us assume it does. Moreover, it seems that congenitally damaged brains (retarded from birth) don't acquire such sophisticated intellectual interests in philosophy, composing, achievement, morality etc. Likewise, damaged brains don't retain their support of such interests and those interests are no more. The demented have lost the "higher" interests and only more childlike interests remain (or the more childlike interests are new).

This loss of critical interests would be especially problematic if Dworkin were right that "A person's right to be treated with dignity, I now suggest, is the right that others acknowledge his genuine critical interests" (236). If I am right about the disease destroying the patient's critical interests and Dworkin is correct on their importance to dignity, then the late term Alzheimer's patient will have undergone a dramatic decline in dignity. More surprising is that late in the disease, such patients lack an interest in a cure. The basis for their critical interests is gone and they lack an experiential interest in a cure when they are infant-like or comatose. This suggests something has gone very wrong in Dworkin's discussion of our interests and dignity.

An Alternative Account of Moral Status

The same reasons that leave me skeptical of those philosophers who defend abortion and infanticide on the grounds that newborns and the unborn lack the interests necessary for a right to life make me skeptical of any view that implies the demented or comatose don't have interests in being cured. I think such philosophers fail to distinguish *something being in an individual's interest* from that *individual taking an interest in something*. Moreover, it is important to realize that there are things in their interests that are contingently so and others that are necessarily so. The contingently so depend upon the idiosyncrasies of the person's development. For instance, Dworkin maintains that "Critical interests are personal ...

not a discovery of a timeless formula, good for all times and places, but as a direct response to our specific circumstances of place, culture and capacity" (206). So critical interests aren't possessed by the mindless or minimally-minded young, and I have argued that the elderly don't retain such interests after disease has eradicated the brain states wherein they were physically realized. Dworkin fails to recognize that we possess necessary as well as contingent interests. Velleman may either not recognize what are necessary interests or wrongly think that they don't matter because they aren't the interests of a rational person.

It is in the fetus's, infant's, comatose and demented's interests to live on even though they may not have taken an interest (i.e., desire) to live further into the future. Analogously, vegetables are in a child's interest even when he's not interested in them. All living things have an interest in healthy development. We can ascribe interests to potential persons, even mindless ones, to live and develop in a healthy fashion by which they will flourish. It may even be that consciousness evolved to promote the same well-being that organisms had previously furthered without awareness of doing so. Regardless, if one doesn't accept that non-sentient beings can have welfare interests then one won't be able to explain the harm of lapsing into a coma or the benefit of coming out of a coma for harms and benefits involve changes from one level of well-being to another, not a move to or from the absence of any well-being.[7]

Even blades of grass can be said to literally thrive and thus have an intrinsic well-being and a non-metaphorical interest in sun and nutrient-rich soil. Despite having interests, a blade of grass has a future that isn't very valuable, so its interests and

[7] There is a difference between the absence of or no well-being on the one hand, and zero or low-level well-being on the other. We were all devoid of any level of well-being, even zero, before we existed and that explains why coming into existence isn't a benefit. The comatose have zero or low well-being, unlike the non-existent and inanimate with well-being.

flourishing are given far less moral weight than those of human beings. Assuming that the degree of the harm of an entity's death depends, in part, upon the value and extent of the well-being that it loses out on, the grass is harmed very little. A healthy human fetus, on the other hand, has the potential to realize mental capacities of considerable value that will enable it to obtain levels of well-being unrivaled by other kinds of creatures. Creatures with minds like ours are liable to obtain greater benefits and suffer greater harms and thus have more value than living things that are not capable of such thoughts and emotions. Even unhealthy fetuses and demented adults have a potential that accounts for their moral status. It may be that the harm is preempted or overdetermined by disease, but then the harm should be considered the combination of the disease and death, what Jeff McMahan calls "Total Harm" and Neil Feit labels "Plural Harm."[8] Killing the incapacitated contributes to the total or plural harm that the patient suffers.

My contention is that the morally relevant sense of potential is determined by what is healthy development for things of that kind. Human fetuses, the retarded and the demented have the potential to develop minds of great cognitive and affective abilities. The healthy realization of these abilities will enable them to enter into various rewarding relationships and exercise a range of cognitive skills that empower them to think and act in valuable ways unlike any other kind of living being. So their potential means that they'll be greatly harmed if deprived of that valuable future. Causing the death of the terminally diseased is being responsible for a component of the overall plural or total harm.

Mindless or minimally minded organisms only have interests in healthy development or proper functioning and the flourishing that involves. So a healthy embryo or retarded

---

[8]Jeff McMahan, *The Ethics of Killing* (2002); Neil Feit, "Plural Harm," *Philosophy and Phenomenological Research*, forthcoming.

child has an interest in growing a healthy proper functioning brain but no interest then in becoming a tennis player even if it will later be an adolescent dreaming of Wimbledon fame. Likewise, the demented no longer have an interest in athletic fame, undertaking philosophy, being independent of care givers, or any other contingent interests that they acquired in their socialization. It isn't enough for mindless or minimally minded entities to be identical to earlier or later rational beings to presently attribute to them the interests that they possess at other times. The earlier or later good must be in the mentally unsophisticated beings' interests when they are mindless or minimally minded. And the only basis I can see for ascribing interests to the mindless is by appealing to the good realized by their proper functioning, i.e., healthy development for entities of that kind. Health is a *necessary* condition for flourishing and constitutive of a good deal of valuable well-being in a healthy person. The living will *always* have an interest in health-produced flourishing. All flourishing depends upon health being present (to some) degree and every living being has an interest in health at every stage of their lives, including their geriatric or embryonic stages. When mindless, there's probably nothing else to their prudential good and flourishing than their health.

The appeal to healthy development as the morally relevant potential renders unnecessary any appeal to the distinction between active and passive potential or the equally problematic intrinsic and extrinsic potential. Anyway, the appeal to active or intrinsic potential wouldn't divide up cases as their proponents want. There's no active or intrinsic potential for (Lockean) personhood in demented adults, anencephalic, or congenitally retarded human fetuses, but they would surely have priority over a healthy kitten to receive a *scarce* serum that made personhood possible for them. So it isn't intrinsically manifested traits in which lies our moral status. Rather, our dignity depends upon the kind of being that we are. As Anscombe wrote, "There is just one impregnable equality of all human beings. It lies in the value and dignity of being a human being" (67).[9]

Once we recognize that the harm of dementia depends upon comparing our present state to the way we should be if we develop in a healthy manner appropriate for our kind, we can easily see why the infant-like demented have greater moral status than any nonhuman animals like cats that might be cognitively equivalent to demented humans. The former are susceptible to a range of serious harms and extraordinary benefits far more significant than anything that cats are susceptible to; so infant-like patients can be the source of stronger reasons for respect and concern than cats can be. The demented's moral status is *raised* above that of cats by their potentiality which depends upon the kind of being that they are. Their dignity lies in the developmental potential of their kind. It is wrong to kill demented humans when they want to go on living even if they have written in their advanced directive to do so. Their interest in their healthy potential doesn't disappear with contingent interests in say sports or literature or philosophy or independence. It is an interest that they always have; it is a necessary condition for flourishing. Babies have it but aren't conscious of it. The demented have the same interest in a return to health but may not realize it. And they preserve that interest even when the destruction of their brain removes any contingent critical interest in ceasing to live when, say, dependent upon others or unable to study science or philosophy or write poetry. If Margo ever had those contingent critical interests, they are gone.

If Margo's moral status was due to her possession of rationality, contingent critical interests or experiential interests, we wouldn't have any grounds based on her interests to cure her of her dementia with a scarce serum rather than make a

[9]Anscombe, G.E.M. "The Dignity of the Human Being." *Human Life, Action and Ethics: Essays by G.E.M. Anscombe.*

cat into a person. But surely we ought to restore personhood to the Alzheimer's patient or bestow it for the first time on the congenitally retarded human beings. They are supposed to be rational persons. That is the kind of entity that they are.

In conclusion, Velleman and Kant are right that your value is the same as others. To disrespect the value in yourself is to disrespect it in others. To disrespect it in others is to devalue it in oneself. A duty not to kill oneself has the same basis as the duty not to kill another. Their mistake is just that they located your value in the wrong place. Anscombe provides the correct diagnosis:

> This lack of reverence, of respect for that dignity of human nature so wonderfully created by God, is the lack of respect for the one impregnable equality of all human beings. Lacking it you cannot revere the dignity of your human-ness that is the dignity of that same human nature in yourself. You may value yourself highly as a tennis player or natural scientist, but without a change of heart you cannot value yourself as being a human, as a *Mensch*. For you have shewn the value you set on a human life as such. You are willing to extinguish it as it suits you or the people who want you to do so. (72)[10]

References

Anscombe, G.E.M. (2005). "The Dignity of the Human Being." *Human Life, Action and Ethics: Essays by G.E.M. Anscombe*. Eds. Luke Gormally and Mary Geach. Imprint Academic.

Dworkin, Ronald. (1993). *Life's Dominion: An Argument about Abortion, Euthanasia and Individual Freedom*. Knopf.

Feit, Neil. "Plural Harm", (2015). *Philosophy and Phenomenological Research*. 90: 361-388.

[10]Ibid. I would like to thank Catherine Nolan for her comments on earlier drafts of this paper.

Hershenov, David. (2005). "Do Dead Bodies Pose a Problem for the Biological Account of Identity?" *Mind*, 114:453. 31-59.

Hershenov, David. (2007). "Death, Dignity and Degradation," *Public Affairs Quarterly*, 21:1. 21-36

Hershenov, David. (2009). "Organisms and their Bodies,"*Mind* 118:70. 803-809.

McMahan, Jeff. (2002). *The Ethics of Killing*. Oxford University Press.

Velleman, David. (1999). "*A Right of Self-Termination?*" *Ethics* 109, 606-628.

6. Dignity, Pet-Euthanasia, and Person-Euthanasia

T. A. Cavanaugh

In "Murder and the Morality of Euthanasia," G.E.M. Anscombe (2005) – in a characteristically intriguing passage – considers dignity and the euthanizing of both humans and other animals. She writes:

> The drive to get doctors killing people and to have this accepted in medical ethics ought to be regarded as sinister even by those who regard suicide in face of terminal suffering as justified and worthy of a human being. If the ground for this opinion is the dignity of human freedom and self-determination, it is inconsonant with this to ask someone else to do so grave a thing. At this point it is often said that people who would kill themselves if they could are rendered unable to do it by physical incapacity. This is less often true than may be supposed, as it is usually possible to stop eating; though the point is not of interest to Christians, who would not be recommending suicide in any form. But with the plea 'Kill me: I need

> death but cannot kill myself' it becomes clear that it is not the dignity of human self-determination that is in question. What is demanded is that such suffering people be treated as we treat the other animals. The impulse 'to put an animal out of its misery' is an impulse of sympathy with a creature that resembles us. The attitude is mistakenly called mercy or care: you cannot take care of something by destroying it. But you can judge it worth not preserving, and sympathy makes it feel indecent to put up with its gross suffering, and may even incline one to terminate a reduced and pathetic existence.
>
> But men, being spirit as well as flesh, are not the same as the other animals. Whatever blasphemes the spirit in man is evil, discouraging, at best trivialising, at worst doing dirt on life. Such is the considered recommendation of suicide and killing in face of suffering. (p. 269)

Here, Anscombe makes a number of thought-provoking claims – almost as asides. In this paper, I develop two.

First, that doctors killing patients (or euthanasia, to be more precisely defined, shortly) is, "inconsonant with," "the dignity of human freedom and self-determination." One cannot ground euthanasia upon dignity insofar as one interprets that, as is customary, in terms of self-determination. For, (Anscombe suggests) self-determination would argue for self-killing (which she clearly opposes, while implying that it, at least on the face of things, comports with self-rule), not being-killed-by-another as occurs in euthanasia. In addressing this point, I consider whether the same holds for a physician's assisting a patient to kill himself, or PAS. (PAS is legal in, e.g., Oregon and Washington. See, for example, "The Oregon Death with Dignity Act," or Oregon Ballot Measure 16 (1994). Washington's legislation follows Oregon's in all important respects.)

The second Anscombian claim I articulate is that euthanasia equates, "suffering people," to other animals undergoing, "gross suffering," whom we decently kill. By contrast, so to kill humans does, in her inimitable words, "dirt on life." Again, I consider whether the same holds for PAS.

Inconsonance of Self-determination with Euthanasia (and PAS)

Consider Anscombe's first point, concerning the jarring juxtaposition of a doctor and the killing of a patient. She (2005) writes:

> The drive to get doctors killing people and to have this accepted in medical ethics ought to be regarded as sinister even by those who regard suicide in face of terminal suffering as justified and worthy of a human being. If the ground for this opinion is the dignity of human freedom and self-determination, it is inconsonant with this to ask someone else to do so grave a thing. (p. 269)

One requires only a passing familiarity with the literature advocating euthanasia and PAS to know that self-determination – also commonly referred to as 'patient autonomy' – almost entirely grounds the arguments for the ethical and legal acceptability of these practices. (For one of the standard arguments, see, e.g., Brock (1992, p. 11).) Thus, Anscombe's point – made almost entirely in passing – has significance. For if she correctly notes that euthanasia clashes with self-determination (and, as I will now argue, so too does PAS), then the principal argument for those practices proves defective. With the import of her claim in mind, let us examine it.

First, let us define our terms. As is customary, by 'euthanasia' I refer (and I understand Anscombe does, also) to voluntary active euthanasia, or VAE. (Henceforth, I will use 'VAE' and 'euthanasia' interchangeably.) VAE refers to that practice by which a physician lethally injects a competent (adequately screened, for example, for clinical depression) terminally ill patient (diagnosed as having six or fewer months to live) at her own considered request. Voluntary active euthanasia contrasts with non-voluntary active euthanasia of a currently incompetent patient. (I address non-voluntary active euthanasia at the end of this paper.)

PAS refers to that practice by which a physician writes a prescription for a lethal drug at the considered request of a patient (relevantly similar to the patient involved in euthanasia) who then fills the prescription and takes the lethal drug when he chooses to do so.[1] For our purposes, the two practices principally differ in terms of who, proximately, causes the death. Clearly, this difference bears on our current concern – the compatibility (or incompatibility) of self-determination with VAE and PAS. Before addressing that topic, consider the terms 'autonomy' and 'self-determination'.

Autonomy refers, of course, to the concept of one's self (in Greek 'autos') as giving the law (in Greek 'nomos') that one follows or in accordance with which one acts. Needless to say, the concept admits of extensive treatment into which I will not enter. Briefly, in the modern intellectual period, one traces it to Immanuel Kant. However, insofar as he emphasizes the

[1] I describe both practices in terms of a successfully completed case. Of course, a patient who opts for PAS need not fill the prescription nor take the drug. However, this fails to illustrate the practice. A patient who does not fill the prescription or one who does not take the prescribed drug does not exemplify PAS just as an unused firecracker does not instance fireworks. That is, just as one does not see fireworks by looking at a firecracker one does not commit (or assist in) PAS by only requesting (or writing) a prescription. Rather, a patient completes an act of PAS when he requests a lethal prescription, receives it, fills it, takes the lethal drug, and, thereby, dies. A patient has not committed PAS nor has a physician assisted a patient's suicide unless a suicide by lethally prescribed drug actually occurs. Moreover, PAS legalizes precisely such an act, not merely the physician's writing or the patient's receipt of a prescription for a lethal drug.

role of reason in the law that one lays down for one's self, his account differs significantly from what many currently mean by autonomy.

As currently employed, 'autonomy' characteristically amounts to something like getting to do what one wants as long as one does not harm others. I take Anscombe's use of 'self-determination' to be closer to what most people actually do mean when they argue for PAS and VAE than a historically accurate Kantian concept of autonomy. Of course, 'self' is an English pronoun denoting the individual while 'determination' comes from the Latin meaning to 'lay down a boundary'. The boundary being the terminus, from 'term' for 'peg' or that which marks the limit of a land parcel. In what follows I will use 'autonomy' and 'self-determination' interchangeably. While there are important differences between the two, I do not take them to be relevant to the current argument.[2]

With the above terminological preliminaries in place, let us turn to consider Anscombe's singular claim that the, "dignity of human freedom and self-determination," do not jibe with VAE. We will then consider the relevance of this claim to PAS. Because it is both what she explicitly maintains and the easier case to make, consider VAE first.

Prima facie (and *ultima facie*, as I now argue) VAE strikes a discordant note with patient autonomy. Indeed, so much so that a number of advocates of PAS oppose VAE as they consider

---

[2]As Kant himself emphasizes, 'autonomy' brings to mind the rule of law and, thereby, of reason as law is a "rule of reason," as Aquinas notes (*Summa theologiae*, IaIIae, q. 90). 'Self-determination', by contrast, brings to mind ownership, the boundaries of one's parcel, and, thereby, one's possessions, one's body, one's life. I am inclined to think that, as the English root 'self' indicates, self-determination is more at issue in, e.g., the U.S. debate concerning PAS and VAE. That is, that the life in question belongs to me and I get to dispose of it as I see fit, as if it were my property. Regardless, the inconsonance remains on either account.

it a threat to autonomy.[3] For in VAE the physician kills the patient. To be put to death by another is not to determine one's own self. Indeed, in VAE another literally determines one's final terminus in various ways including time, place, manner, and so on. Let us consider just one way in which this is true; namely, with respect to when one actually dies. I do so because the time of one's death by definition bears on self-determination as one's death-date is one's terminus. Thus, not to lay this down is definitively not to de-termine one's self.

Imagine the following patient (as advocates of PAS who oppose VAE no doubt do). Call him 'Joe'. Joe has gone through the process to be granted recourse to VAE. Once approved, what comes next for Joe? Well, scheduling a doctor's-appointment, of course. Let us say that Joe decides he wants to be euthanized on his birthday – to bring things full circle, as it were. On his birthday he enjoys himself and feels decent, indeed, euphoric. The doctor arrives; it is time. Yet, Joe does not want to recur to euthanasia right now. What happens? One need not have an overly active imagination to think that this scenario can play out in numerous ways. Consider three. In one case, the doctor shares cake with Joe, Joe's family and friends, and happily reschedules. In another, the physician foregoes cake and grudgingly reschedules. In another scene, Joe reluctantly acquiesces to his own putatively self-determined euthanasia at the hands of a young man in a hurry who has little time for cake and no patience for rescheduling.

Upon brief reflection, one readily understands why both advocates of PAS and Anscombe regard VAE as incongruent with self-determination. Being killed by another – even at one's own request – does not instance self-lawing. Indeed, being killed by another contradicts the self so conceived.

[3]E.g., Timothy Quill, M.D. (1994) considers VAE a threat to patient-autonomy as it puts the act of killing into the physician's hands. Quill advocates PAS; indeed, he (illegally) assisted a patient to kill herself (1991).

Thus, Anscombe's claim concerning the incompatibility of self-rule and VAE stands. Indeed, as noted, advocates of PAS concur with her on this claim – the credibility of which one readily sees.

What of PAS (which Anscombe herself does not address)? Certainly, it appears to harmonize well with an individual's self-government. For in PAS she will be the agent of her own death. In Anscombe's questioning the accuracy of the claim, "'Kill me: I need death but cannot kill myself'," she implies that suicide, literal self-killing (while never to be counseled or countenanced) at least appears to comport with self-sovereignty. The argument above concerning VAE's incompatibility with autonomy does not appear to scathe PAS. So, does PAS congrue with self-rule? Let us now consider this question.

Prima facie, PAS comports with self-determination. For in PAS, unlike VAE, the patient kills herself. The doctor only writes her a prescription for a lethal drug. Indeed, she alone decides whether even to fill the prescription. Having filled it, she decides whether to take the deadly drug. She is the agent of her own demise, she lays down the time, place, witnesses (if any), and contingent circumstances of her death. Unlike Joe, she will not confront a disgruntled young doctor in a hurry were she to change her mind concerning when, where, before whom, or whether she dies by a lethal drug. Presumably, for these and allied reasons, advocates of patient autonomy have greater ease with PAS than with VAE.

Of course, and here we come to the rub between autonomy and PAS, the above picture of PAS, while accurate in all details, lacks salient, less autonomy-friendly features. For, in addition to wanting death competently, the patient must both have and act on account of an acceptable reason. Here we find the opposition Anscombe notes between self-dominion and euthanasia also bearing on PAS.

To see this, consider another patient, Mary. Mary wants a physician's assistance in her self-killing. Following the currently accepted guidelines for PAS (e.g., in the U.S. States of Oregon and Washington), the physician will want to know of Mary if she has adequate medical grounds for wanting to kill herself. So, for example, she must be ill such that her prognosis suggests that she will be dead within six months. Note that if she expects to die within eighteen months, she prematurely wishes to exercise her autonomy. She must wait a year; hardly a robust instance of self-determination.

Further, say that Mary does have a medically acceptable good reason and will, indeed, likely be dead within six months because of a disease (confirmed by two physicians independently, etc). May she be assisted? One would think so. Note, however, that in addition to having the medically acceptable good reason for wanting assistance in killing herself, Mary also must want to kill herself *for this good reason*. More importantly for our purposes, she cannot want to kill herself for a reason that is not medically acceptable. That is, she not only must have the medically acceptable good reason, she must seek out, pursue, and be motivated to kill herself for this reason and not for a non-medical reason. Admittedly, this might seem an odd remark. Allow me to flesh it out.

Say, for example, that in addition to being a terminally ill patient, Mary is an important leader of her people as was Cato who resorted to suicide rather than become a pawn in Caesar's machinations. Were Mary not to kill herself, her nemesis would manipulate her to serve political ends she abhors. For patriotic reasons, Mary wishes to kill herself. Her terminal illness only serves as a convenient cover. Or, perhaps less fantastically, Mary wants to kill herself because she is lonely after her husband Joe's death. A childless widow, Mary wants to kill herself because she is, "horribly alone," and, again, not because she has a terminal illness.

One could go on with permutations of the core example. By now, however, the point ought to be clear. Mary's autonomy does not ground her recourse to PAS. Rather, Mary may recur to PAS only if she determines herself along medically acceptable lines. She may exercise only the autonomy of a patient, not of a self defined in any terms other than those dictated by medicine, physicians, and legislators. In effect, prior to exercising self-determination, she must subordinate herself to all these authorities. Thus, PAS instances a less obvious and, therefore, more insidious medicalization of the self and autonomy than that which occurs in VAE. Indeed, one sees its deceptive character in the rejection of VAE by autonomy-friendly-advocates of PAS who less readily see that it, too, profoundly suborns the self.

Accordingly, Anscombe's point holds concerning the more obvious case of VAE and the initially counter-intuitive case of PAS. Both strike discordantly upon the strings of autonomy. Truly, both, in her remarkable words, "ought to be regarded as sinister even by those who regard suicide in face of terminal suffering as justified and worthy of a human being." If, then, in the plea, "'Kill me: I need death but cannot kill myself'," we do not encounter the, "dignity of human freedom and self-determination," what, precisely, do we face?

Anscombe proposes that we frown upon a request that we treat our fellows, "as we treat the other animals." Is she correct? In contrast to a dignified stoic demand for self-killing, are we looking at a request to be treated as we treat Fido or Tabby? Let us now turn to that topic.

I begin, first, with the analogy often made by proponents between, on the one hand, VAE and PAS and, on the other, the widely accepted practice of animal euthanasia. Ironically, many advocates of euthanasia and PAS enthusiastically liken them to our euthanizing of animals without reflecting on the pejorative implications Anscombe sees (correctly, I argue) in that equation. That is, VAE and PAS trivialize and degrade human lives and deaths by equating them with those of brutes.

The Common Claim

Initially, one might understandably consider Anscombe's claim tendentious. Who other than a staunch opponent of euthanasia would see it as tantamount to our widely accepted practice of animal-euthanasia? Has she not erected a straw-man? Surprisingly, she has not. As will become evident, one finds numerous advocates of VAE and PAS asserting that, in killing them, we treat our dogs and cats better than we treat one another (in not permitting recourse to PAS and VAE).

E.g., consider the words of Timothy Quill, a physician and proponent of PAS who wrote in the *New England Journal of Medicine* (1991) about assisting the suicide of Diane, a terminally ill patient. After publicizing his story about assisting her, Quill (1994) received many letters which, he approvingly notes:

> commented that we treat our pets better than we treat ourselves and our families. We would never allow our pets to be put into a coma so they could die of dehydration over a ten-day period, particularly if they could tell us that they were ready to die. It would be cruel to torture them prior to death. We love them too much to allow this to happen. (p. 113)

Lest one think that Quill's sentiment is unique to U.S. medical doctors, one notes that the Canadian physician Gifford-Jones (2009) proposes that Canadians need:

> to start 'The Society for the Prevention of Cruelty to Humans', an organization that would ask legislators to pass laws similar to those used in Holland and Switzerland where lethal injection is controlled and allowed.

Doctor Gifford-Jones favors the approach of veterinary medicine to end-of-life care, saying:

> if I were allowed a committee to oversee my final hours I'd want a veterinarian to be part of that group. I'm hoping he or she would treat me the same way as Debbie [a polar bear euthanized by zoo-keepers], or a loving pet.

Nor is this attitude exclusive to North Americans or physicians, for that matter. We find A.C. Grayling (2009), a Professor of Applied Philosophy at the University of London, holding that:

> the motive behind efforts ... to have physician-assisted suicide legalised is a simple one: it is a human impulse of kindness, based on the realisation that we are gentler to our pets than to our fellow humans in facilitating an ultimate release from suffering when it is needed.

He considers this a, "scandal."

Again in Britain, we find the animal-rights activist and novelist Brigid Brophy proposing that, "euthanasia is the one exception when we are nicer to animals than we are to humans" (Linzey, 1999, p. 21). Along similar lines, former Australian Senator Peter Baume (2009) holds that it is not fair to prohibit euthanasia to people while not letting, "dogs and horses suffer as we allow humans to."

Finally, we find a (former) registered nurse Ms. Lesley Martin, author of the book *To Die Like a Dog*. In this work, she recounts her act of killing her terminally ill mother for which she served a prison term of 7 ½ months. She subsequently founded a New Zealand group advocating the legalization of euthanasia, organizing a "Dignity Dog Walk" to, "highlight the inconsistencies between the treatment of sick humans and animals. It [being] ... illegal to keep a suffering animal alive, but the reverse ... [applying] ... for people." Ms. Martin notes that, "eight out of ten people that I speak to invariably have a story of their own about a family member and the second thing they say is 'if we treated our dogs like this or other animals like this, we'd be in court'" (Wood, 2009).

Clearly, as the above quotes from physicians (some who have practiced PAS), a professor of applied philosophy, a novelist, an animal-rights' advocate, a legislator, and an actual euthanizer (and former R.N.) indicate, Anscombe has identified a mentality operative amongst those who propose (and some who practice) PAS and VAE. She has not fashioned a straw-man. Proponents actually do consider the comparison of animal-euthanasia to VAE and PAS as casting a favorable light upon the latter practices.

The tendency of advocates to offer our customary treatment of dying animals as an argument for PAS and VAE deserves consideration, if only because of the frequency and apparent naturalness with which the analogy comes to their minds. Do we treat our pets better than our fellow humans as they lay dying? Do we need a society for the prevention of cruelty to humans to insure they receive the options of PAS and VAE at the end of life? Ought we to be in court for not euthanizing our family members? Do we love our pets more than ourselves and our families? Or, by contrast, as Anscombe contends, do VAE and PAS trivialize the gravity of homicide while treating persons like dogs and, thereby, do, "dirt on life"?

Pet-Euthanasia

Given both the widespread familiarity with pet-euthanasia and the noted tendency to employ that experience in support of PAS and VAE, in what follows I focus on pet-euthanasia.[4] Along the lines suggested by Anscombe, a deeper consideration of the decency of animal euthanasia

---

[4]Lest my comments seem unaware of their own parochiality, I note that they bear on a first-world context. *Mutatis mutandis*, the same points could be made in other contexts; however, and importantly, those things in need of changing would need to be changed.

has troubling implications for the supposed humaneness of PAS and VAE.

Very briefly, consider the history leading up to our widespread acceptance of pet-euthanasia.[5] Thanks to the efforts of individuals such as William Wilberforce – a member of parliament in the late-eighteenth and early-nineteenth centuries, fierce opponent of slavery, devout Christian, and one of the original founders of the Society for the Prevention of Cruelty to Animals (SPCA) – we have come to regard the infliction of unjustified pain upon animals as wrongful, even deserving of punishment. (For more on the admirable Wilberforce, see Metaxas (2007)). While considering the killing of animals for food as legitimate, society has come to abhor gratuitous harm to animals. The SPCA was founded in 1824 partially to support and enforce an 1822 act of the British parliament preventing the cruel treatment of cattle. Of course, we often violate norms against cruelty to animals in, for example, factory-farming practices such as confining animals to cages no larger than themselves. Although much animal-husbandry falls short of our ideals, many societies legally forbid wanton cruelty to animals, especially the more common pets such as dogs and cats.

While such statutes prohibiting cruelty to animals do not positively require that people alleviate their pain, those who have pets and many others have come to abhor allowing a pet to undergo pain at the end of life. Accordingly, this has led to the widespread humane practice of euthanizing a pet at the end of its life, or mercy killing (in, e.g., the U.S.).[6] What does

---

[5]Some question people's readiness to euthanize a pet. For a thoughtful reflection on the tendency of some to euthanize a pet prematurely and its import for treatment of the disabled, see Andre (2003).

[6]I agree with Anscombe that one cannot care for a pet (or anything, for that matter) by destroying it. However, one can by killing it thereby act with a qualified (metaphorical but nonetheless real) mercy towards it. Care and mercy differ. Care sustains a being and is, therefore, incompatible with destruction of that entity. Mercy involves a heart-felt (*cor*, Latin for 'heart') feeling of

this practice indicate about our regard for animals? In what follows, I attend to four salient implications of this custom.

First, implicitly present in pet-euthanasia one finds that we consider animals subordinate beings towards whom we have obligations. We can be good or bad pet-owners. 'Owner', however, does not precisely capture the relationship between the pet and the person. For, unlike ownership of a thing, such as a car, the owner may not ethically or legally treat the pet however she wants. The pet, unlike the car, is a moral and legal patient; it admits of being treated unethically and illegally. Indeed, were its owner to treat the animal cruelly, in many jurisdictions she would be subject herself to fines, the loss of the pet, and even to criminal penalties, including incarceration. (In many jurisdictions in the U.S., animal cruelty amounts to a felony, subject to a year or more in jail.) Perhaps it would be better to speak of the person as a steward or guardian of the pet to convey that she does not exercise absolute dominion over it. While she does not exercise ownership over the pet as she does over things, the pet does belong to her. She may determine what becomes of it, within the ethical and legal boundaries of being a good caretaker. That she ought (in some circumstances) euthanize her pet indicates her dominion over it.

---

sorrow (*miserum*) at the harm another suffers. Hence, in Latin, *misericordia* or sorrowful-heart. Indeed, her statement that, "sympathy makes it feel indecent to put up with its gross suffering," suggests that she is amenable to considering what goes on in animal euthanasia correct affectively It is a sympathetic, decent, humane, and, I would say, tender-hearted, merciful act towards the being that cannot rise above pain and distress such that, for it, what it bears always remains gross suffering. Speaking most precisely, one can exercise the charity mercy instances only towards another human being. However, metaphorically, we can and do correctly speak of mercy towards animals. This includes mercy-killing of pets. For a consideration of the treatments of charity and mercy upon which these comments depend, especially the metaphorical character of the mercy we show towards pets, see Aquinas, *Summa theologiae*, IIaIIae, q. 25, a.3 (regarding the metaphorical character) and q. 30, a.1. (for the specific treatment of mercy).

Second, pet-euthanasia suggests that we do not regard the pet's declination and death as valuable to the pet (or to anyone else, for that matter). That is, we act well, decently, worthily in killing the animal, in taking measures to end its, "reduced and pathetic existence." We correctly consider the pet's pain, symptoms, and distress as entirely negative, to be foreshortened and avoided. The pet gains nothing from its experience of death. It is, in Anscombe's words, "gross suffering." Why?

The pet's suffering is gross because the brute animal naturally cannot rise above and reflect upon what it bears. Instead, we find the pet entirely immersed in its pain and afflictions. Accordingly, the pet has nothing to gain, no new insights to derive from experiencing its own mortality. In fact, it does not experience its own mortality; it simply labors under a burden. Unlike the pet, we understand this burden and its name: mortality.

The poet Gerard Manley Hopkins, S.J. imagines a young child Margaret sorrowing over, "Goldengrove unleaving,": "It ís the blight man was born for, It is Margaret you mourn for" (1985, in the poem entitled *Spring and Fall*). Similarly, when our dog dies, we grieve both at our own loss of the beloved dog's life and at the dog's loss of life (and, thus, we experience mercy metaphorically). The animal, however, remains dumb and mute even at the end of its life, a terminus that it neither comprehends nor contemplates. Indeed, partially for this reason, it is pathetic. It merits pity. No good can come of the animal's endurance of its ending. In light of this we humanely kill a pet whose life holds no prospects for growth as it ends.

Third, just as the animal cannot rise above its own mortality, it cannot kill itself. This follows as a close corollary to the second point and instances another salient element in the pitiable character of the animal's wordless suffering that partially justifies pet-euthanasia. The pet is the kind of being that cannot effect, bring about, or cause its own death. Indeed, its inability to kill itself flows from its incapacity to understand and, thereby, transcend its own death. The possibility of outstripping its mortality by causing its own death remains out of the pet's reach. Its being the kind of being that cannot kill itself partially renders our killing of it decent when, otherwise, it would suffer dumbly.

Fourth, and finally, in euthanizing a dog we also find an intimation of the replaceability of the dog. I struggle to make this point; language does not precisely capture the idea I hope to convey. On the one hand, a dog is not a thing such as a car that (when destroyed) we replace with an identical thing. On the other hand, it is not a person, an entirely irreplaceable and non-fungible being. Simply put, persons cannot be exchanged. A person's death instances an irretrievable loss. Pets fall somewhere between the exchangeability of things and the uniqueness of persons. Pets are, in large part, replaceable. Their replaceability reflects, not the shallowness of our capacity for relationships with animals, but, rather, the appropriate way of relating to pets. Thus, euthanizing an animal suggests the nature of the animal's life as, for the most part, fungible.[7]

In summation, we euthanize our pets as an act of (metaphorical) mercy towards 1) subordinate beings in light of their dual inability 2) by reflection to derive any further benefit from or 3) to themselves end 4) a replaceable life now characterized by pain and distress. How does this custom and these reasons for it relate to VAE and PAS? As noted, many take animal-euthanasia as an obvious analogy justifying VAE and PAS. One might put their point thus: "since we humanely kill

[7]A personal anecdote illustrates the point. Upon the death of our family dog, my parents acquired another dog of the same breed, giving it the same name. My siblings and I quickly overcame our adolescent sorrow at the death of our beloved dog and immediately fell in love with our new pet. By contrast, had we lost a sibling, our parents could not simply replace him or her with another person. For persons cannot be exchanged, one for another, while animals, albeit not entirely fungible, largely share in the replaceable nature of things.

our pets who do not request euthanasia, all the more ought we to kill (or assist) our loved ones who at times actually request us to do so."

Pet-Euthanasia's Import for VAE and PAS

In what follows, I argue that the four above-noted reasons in accordance with which we appropriately euthanize pets do not apply to persons such that we would aptly resort to VAE and PAS. I now articulate and reflect upon these four bases for justified animal-euthanasia and their deficiency *vis-à-vis* justifying VAE and PAS. I do so in the following order: first, inferiority of the killed; second, irreflexivity or immersion in sensation; third, inability to kill self; and fourth, fungibility.

First, when we consider the pet's subordination indicated by our euthanizing it we confront Anscombe's point concerning the implicit degradation of humans present in VAE and PAS. The properly ordered killing of any other being (plant, animal, or human) depends upon the killed somehow being below, subordinate, for the sake of, or defective to the killer. One does not justifiably kill another's exact equal. Thus, for the killing of a human to be just, some superiority must exist between the killer and the justly killed, be it that the killer does not (unjustly) threaten while the killed does (in self-defense), or the killer is the whole (the state) while the killed has acted unjustly and is a part (in the death penalty), etc. Put in other words, in a just killing the killed is less than the killer.

Animals are below us; at times, we justly kill them. Pet-euthanasia instances such a killing. Because the euthanizing of a human would constitute an erroneous subordination of one human to another, we must reject it. For it betrays the radical equality of all humans. While I do not wish to sound alarmist, one notes that the Nazis euthanized people whom they regarded as defective and, thereby, "unworthy of life," (in German, *lebensunwerten Lebens* (Friedlander, 1995, p. 81)). This way of speaking indicates that the Nazis regarded the subject, an individual human being, as not being worthy of the property of being alive. The killing of a human tends to incorporate such a sentiment. The same point holds for assisting in another's killing. One must judge the life of the one whom we assist in self-killing as meriting death and, thereby, as below our own life which we (of course) preserve. (For a consideration of the precedents to the Nazi program of euthanasia, see Friedlander (1995); see also, Burleigh (1994), pp. 11-90. For the bearing of the Nazi euthanasia program on the current debate, see Cavanaugh (1997).)

Second, as noted, animals, unlike humans, cannot significantly reflect upon their own experience. I do not wish to deny that we humans share many important similarities with our pets. (Indeed, our similarities ground our relationships with them.) Those who would deny thinking or communicating or emoting to animals insufficiently know and appreciate animals and their abilities. We differ most pronouncedly with animals not in what we do and what they do not do, but, rather, in what we do concerning what we do and in what they do not do concerning what they do. In other words, our own acts themselves provide extensive material for our further actions while animals do little and some nothing at all respecting their own actions. We might say that while both we and animals are conscious and act as conscious beings do (sense, desire, emote, communicate, think) we also have robust consciousness about our consciousness. We, unlike they, have deep self-consciousness and all that this entails: beliefs about beliefs, desires about desires, knowledge about knowledge, and, most generally, actions concerning our actions.

For the purposes of this paper, most importantly, we, unlike they, can rise above our own deaths, contemplate them, and derive benefits and insights from them. We can contemplate and attempt to understand our own mortality, sickness, pain, suffering, and impending deaths. This truth about us dramatically contrasts animal from human dying. For an animal's death holds out no potential insights for it. By contrast, our deaths promise opportunities available to us only at the end of life. (Indeed, as the passage from Hopkins indicates, we, as does Margaret, learn from the deaths of all living things, even a tree-grove's loss of leaves.)

In the words of Ira Byock, M. D. (1997) (a hospice physician and past President of the American Academy of Hospice and Palliative Medicine), we have, "prospects for growth at the end of life."[8] Animals do not; in part, for this reason, we justifiably euthanize them. Because we can and animals cannot make sense of pain, distress, and the ending of life, we cannot extrapolate from justified animal-euthanasia to the euthanizing of humans. What one does appropriately to a pet one errs in doing to a fellow human – even at that fellow's request.

As an elaboration upon this point, consider Kant's famous analysis of suicide. In his *Groundwork for the Metaphysics of Morals*, Kant proposes that one who resorts to suicide errs. For, Kant says:

> If he destroys himself in order to escape from a difficult situation, then he is making use of his person merely as a means so as to maintain a tolerable condition till the

---

[8]In his extensive experience as a hospice physician, Byock proposes that growth occurs typically in a dying person's request for forgiveness, granting forgiveness, expressing both gratitude and love, and, finally, saying goodbye (1997; see also, Byock, 2004). Amongst other reasons for opposing PAS and VAE, Byock thinks that such practices would dramatically curtail these opportunities. Moreover, the practices would do so unnecessarily, as we can adequately manage pain and symptoms at the end of life, even, if necessary, sedating patients to manage otherwise intractable pain (terminal sedation). Byock (1997, pp. 209-216) recounts the passing of one of his patients who required palliative sedation – the use of which he endorses.

> end of his life. Man, however, is not a thing and hence not something to be used merely as a means; he must in all his actions always be regarded as an end in himself. (1993, p. 36)

No doubt, Kant misunderstands the distraught situation of many in despair who resort to suicide. Consider not that deficiency in his account, however, but, rather, how his analysis bears on VAE and PAS when proposed as rational solutions to distress at the end of life.

Kant understands putative rational human suicide as involving the mistake of regarding one's life only as a means to pleasure. The account (which Kant rightly rejects) holds that once one's life lacks pleasure, or involves too much suffering, burdensome symptoms, and the loss of control over one's bodily functions, one may destroy one's self (or be destroyed by another). We find such thinking present in right opinions about pet-euthanasia and mistaken ones concerning VAE and PAS.

Certainly, this represents how we correctly think about euthanizing our pets. Typically, sensory experience constitutes the entirety of their consciousness. Once that is onerous and not likely to improve, we kill them. To do so acknowledges their actual relationship to sensual pleasure. Basically, their lives merit preservation to the extent to which they contain pleasure. My dog is, literally, a pleasure-hound. Were his life devoid of pleasure, he would no longer be what he is; at that time I will mercifully take his life.

Because dogs in the throes of death cannot comprehend pain and thereby get beyond it, we appropriately kill them when so immersed. We err profoundly, however, when we propose thus to act concerning humans who by nature do rise above pain and thereby transcend it, showing that their lives are not the sum of their sensations.

Third, humans, unlike pets, can kill themselves. Here we register a signal difference between the plight of the animal we mercifully kill and that of those to be killed via PAS and VAE. Namely, as Anscombe notes, the characteristic falsity of the plea: "'Kill me: I need death but cannot kill myself'." Many who would have recourse to VAE actually can (otherwise) kill themselves – similarly, for PAS. More importantly for the present purposes, as beings of certain kinds, humans can and animals cannot kill themselves. (Shortly, I will address this point as it bears on those humans who occurrently cannot kill themselves.)

Fourth, and finally, the (for the most part) fungible character of animal life indicated by euthanasia suggests that the practice does not comport with human dignity. For by 'dignity' we attempt to capture the notion of humans as irreplaceable, without price. Dignity excludes replaceability. The life of a being that has dignity cannot be exchanged for another being and, for this reason, neither can it be taken in exchange for the cessation of pain and distress.[9]

---

[9]Of course – as Anscombe herself clearly indicates elsewhere (and as noted previously in the reference to the physician Ira Byock's recourse to palliative or terminal sedation in the care of terminally ill patients) – we can honor our commitment never to euthanize while also taking aggressive measures to relieve pain and distress at the end of life, even when doing so does effect death concomitantly as a foreseen but not intended side effect. Here is Anscombe (1981, pp. 54-55) on palliative sedation (which she endorses as ethical):

> And in the case of the administration of a pain-relieving drug in mortal illness, where the doctor knows the drug may very well kill the patient if the illness does not do so first, the [I/F] distinction is evident; the lack of it has led an English judge to talk nonsense about the administration of the drug's not having *really* been the cause of death in such a case, even though a post mortem shows it was." (original emphasis)

Of course, terminal sedation instances a classic case of double effect – concerning the development of which Anscombe serves as a central contemporary figure. On double effect's use in end-of-life care and more generally, see Cavanaugh (2006).

The most incompetently alive

As noted, points two and three above concerning humans' ability, unlike pets, to comprehend their own suffering and to effect their own deaths bring up an earlier mooted point concerning humans who here and now (or, occurrently) can neither contemplate their own deaths nor kill themselves. As we will see, Anscombe refers to such persons as, "the most incompetently alive." Perhaps we ought to euthanize such persons as we do our pets who can neither kill themselves nor rise above their own deaths to comprehend them? (Obviously, the question does not arise concerning PAS.) Before concluding, I want to address euthanasia as it bears on people so situated.

There is a lot of territory to treat of here; space does not permit an extensive treatment of the relevant issues. I do, however, want to limn an argument. Before doing so, one must distinguish different forms of euthanasia. Thus far we have been speaking of VAE, voluntary active euthanasia that concerns a currently competent patient. By contrast, non-voluntary active euthanasia concerns three categories of patients similar to the VAE-patient, but for competency. First, we have the once-competent but now no longer competent person who previously asked us to euthanize him. Second, we have the once but now no longer competent person who never opined concerning euthanasia one way or the other. Third, we have the never-competent person.

Concerning all three I have two points. First, each is a human being, and, thereby, a person (an individual of a rational nature) equal to any and all other human persons.[10] That which belongs to a human being belongs to each of them. In this respect the three noted patients do not importantly differ

---

[10]Aquinas, *S.t.*, Ia, q. 29, a.1, approvingly quoting Boethius, "*persona est rationalis naturae individua substantia.*"

from a currently competent patient while they radically differ from a pet. This essential characteristic they all have: they are equally human. For this reason, not one of them can be regarded without serious (ontological/metaphysical) error as adequately similar to the dog euthanized appropriately, in light of its nature. This holds without respect to their disabilities – occasional or permanent. Indeed, to cite a person's inability as a basis for killing him adds grievous insult to the injury that incapacity instances in his life. Only a being to whom, e.g., understanding naturally belongs can suffer from the absence of understanding. One perversely singles such a person out for killing rather than caring.

Second – and I will conclude my treatment of this topic with this point – that a person lives with or without consciousness itself indicates that person's desire to live. Consider Anscombe's observation in the same paper from which our topic arises:

> The human heart and will are set on amenity; they may also be set on what is just: that is (when it comes to dying) set in acceptance of life — which is God's gift – and of death, as it comes from him. This goes even for the most incompetently alive in whom the will is manifested mainly in the vital operations. (2005, p. 270)

Elsewhere, Anscombe (2000, p. 68) famously says that the, "primitive sign of wanting is trying to get." Can we not, with her, assert that even the, "most incompetently alive," do want to live and evidence their desire by living? To deny the evidence of this desire is to embrace a dubious dichotomous duality between body and psyche.

Paraphrasing Pascal's, "*le cœur a ses raisons, que la raison ne connaît point*" (1963, p. 552) may we not say that, "the body has its reasons which reason does not understand"? Certainly, the readiness of some to kill humans incapable of performing characteristically human acts depends upon a metaphysics that does not withstand scrutiny. For it reduces the real to what occurs, thereby denying kinds. With this (admittedly brief) treatment of the, "most incompetently alive," let us conclude.

In summation, what conclusions do the preceding arguments warrant?[11] Three merit repetition. First, both VAE and PAS do not comport with self-determination. Second, both practices equate a person to a pet. Third, so to equate a grandmother, grandfather, father, mother, uncle, aunt, wife, husband, son, daughter, sister, brother, niece, nephew, cousin, friend, neighbor, stranger, or any fellow human being with a dog or cat both trivializes human death and does dirt on human life.

[11]Respecting what has not been shown, two points bear remark. First, neither this paper nor Anscombe's own comments show suicide to be incompatible with self-determination broadly construed. Second, both this paper and Anscombe's comments that prompt it imply that this needs to be shown. For, *prima facie*, suicide seems compatible with autonomy. I note in passing, however, that in diverse times and places we find highly regarded secular thinkers – such as Socrates and Jefferson – broadly rejecting self-killing so as to exclude PAS and VAE while at the same time evidencing sympathy, even championing self-rule. While Socrates would not be entirely at home with the individualism latent in modern conceptions of self-government, Jefferson can certainly be counted amongst its advocates. In *Phaedo*, Socrates holds that even in dire straits – such as his condemnation to death by the Athenians – one ought not to kill oneself. For one's life is not entirely one's own (Plato, *Phaedo*, lines 61c-62d.). Over two millennia later, we find Jefferson writing of, "inalienable rights," in the *Declaration of Independence*, amongst which he numbers the right to life. Of course, an inalienable right cannot be separated from the individual, not even by the individual him or herself. Thus, according to the account Jefferson advances and that one finds at the founding of the U.S. Republic, one may not legitimately kill oneself.

References

Andre, L. (2003). Disability culture meets euthanasia culture: lessons from my cat. *Disability Studies Quarterly*, 23 (3/4).

Anscombe, G. E. M. (1981). War and murder. In Anscombe, *The collected philosophical papers of G. E. M. Anscombe* (Vol. 3) (pp., 51-61). Oxford, UK: Basil Blackwell.

Anscombe, G. E. M. (2000). *Intention* (2nd ed.). Cambridge, MA: Harvard University Press.

Anscombe, G. E. M. (2005). Murder and the morality of euthanasia. In Geach, M., & Gormally, L. (Eds.), *Human life, action and ethics: essays by G. E. M. Anscombe* (pp. 261-277). Exeter, UK: Imprint Academic; St. Andrews Studies in Philosophy and Public Affairs.

Aquinas, Thomas (1962). *Summa theologiae. Roma, IT: Editiones Paulinae.*

Baume, P. (2009, February 4). *The Sydney Morning Herald.*

Brock, D. (1992). Voluntary active euthanasia. *The Hastings Center Report*, 22 (2), 10-22.

Burleigh, M. (1994). *Death and deliverance:"euthanasia" in Germany 1900-1945*. Cambridge, UK: Cambridge University Press.

Byock, I. (1997). *Dying well: prospects for growth at the end of life*. New York, NY: Riverhead.

Byock, I. (2004). *The four things that matter most: a book about living*. New York, NY: Free Press.

Cavanaugh, T. A. (1997). The *Nazi!* accusation and current U.S. proposals. *Bioethics*, 11 (3/4), 291-297.

Cavanaugh, T. A. (2006). *Double-effect reasoning: doing good and avoiding evil*. Oxford, UK: Clarendon.

Friedlander, H. (1995). *The origins of nazi genocide: from euthanasia to the final solution*. Chapel Hill, NC: The University of North Carolina Press.

Gifford-Jones, W. (2009, February 7). *The Toronto Sun*, p. 27.

Grayling, A. C. (2009, March 31). *The Times* (London), p. 26.

Hopkins, G. M. (1985). *Gerard Manley Hopkins: poems and prose*. New York, NY: Penguin, p. 50.

Jefferson, T. (1776). *Declaration of Independence.*

Kant, I. (1993). *Grounding for the metaphysics of morals.* (J. Ellington, Trans.). Indianapolis, IN: Hackett.

Linzey, A. (1999). Worse than death. *The Animals' Agenda*, 19 (4).

Metaxas, E. (2007). *Amazing grace: William Wilberforce and the heroic campaign to end slavery*. New York, NY: Harper Collins.

Oregon Ballot Measure 16. (1994).

Pascal, B. (1963). *Pensées*. In *Œuvres complètes* (pp. 493-641). Paris, FR: Macmillan, *Éditions du Seuil.*

Plato (2002). *Phaedo*. In *Five dialogues* (pp. 93-154). (G.M.A. Grube, Trans.). Indianapolis, IN: Hackett.

Quill T. (1991). Death and dignity – a case of individualized decision making. *New England Journal of Medicine*, 324, pp. 691–694.

Quill, T. (1994). *Death and dignity*. New York, NY: Norton.

Wood, S. (2009, May 16). *The Dominion Post* (Wellington, New Zealand), p. 6.

7. Anscombe, Abortion, and Human Dignity

Ryan Cobb

I hope to accomplish two tasks in this paper[1]. First, I want to elaborate Anscombe's rather terse reasoning against abortion. Second, I hope to defend her position by considering several objections against it. (The reader should note that I am only attempting to outline and defend an "Anscombian" argument—an argument inspired by Anscombe's comments and relatively faithful to Anscombe's text. I make no claim to offer an authoritative account of her argument.)

I shall focus on Anscombe's (2005) essay "The Dignity of the Human Being," wherein she describes human dignity and some violations of it as a means of explaining what is wrong with abortion. Here's Anscombe in her own words:

---

[1]I would like to thank T. Cavanaugh, M. Cobb, and G. Stoutenburg for their help in preparing this paper. I would also like to thank all the participants of the Anscombe Forum for improving this paper in ways that are difficult to attribute. Finally, I would like to thank the organizers of the Anscombe Forum and Neumann University for their hospitality.

> [Human dignity is] violated in chattel slavery where the slave had no rights . . . It is violated every time people are killed for others' convenience . . . or when anyone murders his fellow human, not in anger as deserving death, but for advantage to himself. So too it is violated when an obviously human foetus [sic] is deliberately killed in abortion. It is violated by someone who puts his dead or dying mother out into a rubbish bin. (pp. 67-8)

Here is one (hopefully plausible) interpretation of Anscombe's argument:

1) Violations of human dignity are wrong.
2) Abortion is a violation of human dignity.
3) Thus, abortion is wrong.

Let's take up the premises in order.

Regarding premise one, three questions arise. What is human dignity? What are violations of human dignity? Why think that violations of human dignity are wrong in themselves?

Human dignity is, *prima facie*, the respect due to human beings *qua* human beings. If you're a human being, you merit certain kinds of treatment. Anscombe suggests that proper respect for the dying is part of human dignity, giving us the example of putting one's dead or dying mother out with the trash as an (obvious) violation (p. 68). (Note that there might be more than one reason for not doing so. Assuming that this action is a violation of human dignity and such violations are wrong, the action seems wrong for several other reasons. One's mother deserves special consideration, or you might have made a promise that you would not treat her in this way, etc. But the point is that even if we have no other reasons against the action, the action is still wrong—it violates human dignity.) We owe other human beings a certain level of respect *in virtue of* their being human beings. Alternatively, we might think of human dignity in Kantian terms: human beings are ends-in-themselves, and must never be treated merely as means to a further end. I am hesitant about using Kant's language here, as Kant (1964) thinks only rational agents are ends in themselves, and I want to include all human beings as having human dignity. Adapting Kant somewhat, Kant gets it right that you can't "use" people; he merely gets the extension of people wrong.

There is a worry lurking in the background here. Isn't this just speciesism—claiming that humans deserve special treatment *qua* humans, with no further reason? [2] Not quite. I am not arguing that humans alone have dignity or should be treated with respect. Humanity is *sufficient* for being treated with respect, but not necessary. So, it seems to me to be wrong to put Koko the gorilla out with the trash, too, but certainly not because she is human—or, because she meets some vague concept of "person."

Again, then, we must ask—what, exactly, is a violation of human dignity? I have two kinds of violations in mind here, although there is probably overlap. First, any action that treats someone merely as a tool for our use is such a violation. Think about criticisms of pornography that contend that it treats women as "sex objects" (Garry 1978). The idea is, I think, that pornography treats its "subjects" as though they have no value to the consumer of pornography except as a tool for sexual arousal. This kind of objectification, I contend, is wrong because it violates human dignity. (It is a separate question whether pornography in fact objectifies women, and if so, whether this is inherent in the notion of pornography itself. I shall not chase this particular rabbit here.) Note that the objectification need not be sexual. To use a silly example, suppose I use a roommate's teeth as a beer bottle opener while

---

[2]Following Peter Singer's usage of the term in his *Animal Liberation* (1975).

he sleeps. This kind of action treats him merely as an object for my use and thereby violates his dignity.

A second way of violating human dignity is via "commodification." (Note, however, that it isn't clear that commodification forms a partition with "objectification." So, we might say that the producers of pornography "commodify" women (and men), as well as objectify. So it isn't clear there are separate ways of behaving here. Perhaps by treating someone merely as a tool, we allow him to be commodified, or vice versa. But I will not trouble the distinctions too much here.) By "commodification", I mean treating a thing that has more than economic value in purely economic terms. Suppose I own a beautiful painting. I have it appraised, and it is worth hundreds of thousands of dollars. A wealthy art collector offers me double its appraised value, but warns me that if I sell, he will destroy the painting (he hates the artist and seeks to destroy all of his work). Should I accept the offer? Untangling all the threads of that question is a difficult task. But, in short, I say "no." I ought to refuse such an offer because there is more value to the painting than its price, and to allow its destruction for purely financial reasons is to "commodify" the painting. (Incidentally, I think this is why I find the concept of buying art pieces as an investment odd and a bit distasteful. Can't the "investor" see anything beyond the dollar sign?) Of course the painting *is* a commodity—it may be bought and sold; it has a cash value. But the painting is more than a commodity. (Think of the recent ISIS destruction of ancient artifacts. Is anyone upset about this because the destroyed items *are expensive*?)

Human beings are also much more than commodities. It is wrong to treat them as though they have (merely) economic value. Why? Because to commodify is to violate human dignity—it is to fail to respect a human *qua* human. This is (partly) why it is wrong to suppose that it is all right to kill anyone you wish, so long as you pay his family whatever a fair life insurance policy would pay. It is not just that you have violated his autonomy or caused great torment for his family (although you have), it is that you are considering him purely in economic terms. To give another example, it is the difference between a factory owner and potential employee negotiating as equals over pay, and the same owner treating the worker as nothing but cattle. It is not merely whether the worker is bargaining from a position of strength. It is how the factory owner considers him: if he is a man who must be respected, the owner has acknowledged his human dignity. If the owner treats him as merely a (valuable) piece of machinery, the owner has violated his human dignity.

So we have at least two ways of violating human dignity (which, again, may not form a partition—it is possible, I suppose, that an action could violate human dignity in both ways). But an objection might be that I have characterized the phenomenon inaccurately. What these "violations" *really are*—so the objection goes—are violations of autonomy. And, note that one must be autonomous to have one's autonomy violated. And, if autonomy is the relevant issue, this preempts our argument against abortion, for it sounds *prima facie* implausible to say that abortion violates the autonomy of fetuses.[3] So, the objection goes, the whole argument has started off on the wrong foot. However, I think this objection has the stick by the wrong end—violations of human dignity are the genus, and violations of autonomy merely a species. Thus, it is possible to violate the dignity of humans without violating their autonomy. We can see that violations of autonomy are a class of violations of human dignity by considering the following. First, note that violations of human dignity

---

[3]Of course, one may say that one has violated a fetus's future autonomy; or perhaps, violated its autonomy by denying it the ability to develop autonomy. This is a defensible position, and one could perhaps mount an anti-abortion argument in this fashion. But this is outside the scope of the current argument. We must leave it to one side.

can occur without violating autonomy. We find something repulsive about selling one's mother's body to cannibals or necrophiliacs. It is unclear whether there is any *autonomy* to violate here—it seems your dead mother has none—but there is still a violation of human dignity. Second, it is difficult to point out what is wrong with violating autonomy *without* appealing to human dignity. Simply saying something is an autonomous being is no good unless we think it is the kind of thing we should respect. Pet owners violate their pets' autonomy all the time, but this is not wrong. It is not clear we must respect autonomous beings *qua* autonomous beings unless we have some clear notion of personhood we wish to defend. That is, it isn't clear why being autonomous makes one worthy of certain moral consideration, unless we have some idea of a moral person that crucially depends on autonomy. Relying on human dignity allows us to sidestep the sticky wicket of personhood.

If we have some idea of what human dignity is, and what it is to violate it, why think that it is wrong to violate human dignity? That is (borrowing another notion from Anscombe (1957)), supposing there is some description under which some actions fall (violations of human dignity), why think that this category of action is wrong? Here I find myself relying on, to use a phrase that has generated much contemporary philosophical buzz, an intuition. But I think my intuition is reliable, and I have relied on example to pump your intuitions, as well. In short, I am not sure that I can do much to defend the wrongness of violations of human dignity, other than to describe some cases that fall under that description and hope that you agree.

Let's move to a discussion of the argument's second premise: abortion is a violation of human dignity. How shall we attempt to prove this, or what could amount to a proof of it? Let's see what Anscombe says:

> So a woman of today may find a possibility of becoming pregnant, letting the baby grow to twenty eight weeks (because bigger ones are worth more) and then going somewhere where they will pay her for a late abortion, which yield the foetus [sic] for resale, say, as valuable material. If you act so, are not shewing [sic] that you do not regard that human being with any reverence? Few will fail to see that. But the same is true of one who has an abortion so that she can play in a tennis championship; or for any reason for which someone might choose to destroy the life of a new human being . . . [Y]ou have shewn [sic] the value you set on a human life as such. You are willing to extinguish it as suits you or as suits the people who want you to do so. (2005, p. 72)

Anscombe seems to have the following argument in mind for a defense of premise two:

> Abortions for certain frivolous reasons violate human dignity, but if we allow abortion generally we must allow abortion for these frivolous reasons, so abortion *qua* abortion violates human dignity. We can represent Anscombe's argument in the following schema.
>
> 4) If x is morally permissible, then y is, in principle, morally permissible.
> 5) y is a violation of human dignity.
> 6) Any action that in principle makes a violation of human dignity morally permissible is itself a violation of human dignity.
> 7) Therefore, x is a violation of human dignity.

There are two steps to successfully advance this argument. First, 6) is in need of some defense. Second, we must find an x and y such that y is a violation of human dignity, x makes y in principle permissible, etc.

Let's begin by defending 6). It relies on a more fundamental principle—call it P. For any wrong action A, there is some reason why it is wrong. But if some other action B is such that it is wrong for the same reason A is, we must say that both A and B are wrong (or, possibly, change our minds and allow both A and B). (Of course, we might think that there is some additional reason that makes A or B wrong, in which case A could be wrong without B being wrong or *vice versa*. I will not consider such cases here.)

An example might help illustrate P. Suppose we want to know whether a pre-emptive nuclear strike is ever permissible. Suppose further that someone contends that there is nothing inherently wrong with such an action—it requires no special justification. It might be wrong for some other reason—say, if one has promised not to do so—but there is no moral difficulty with the act itself. One might argue against this position along these lines. If a pre-emptive nuclear strike is permissible, then it is permissible to perform such a strike to test one's nuclear capabilities, which seems insane. That is, if we suppose that a pre-emptive nuclear strike is morally unproblematic, then it would be unreasonable to contend that we couldn't strike just to test our capabilities. If an action in itself is not morally objectionable, then it does not matter what one's reasons are for doing it.[4] And, further, if we decide that pre-emptive

[4]Unless, of course, this introduces some further objectionable element. So, it may be morally unproblematic in itself to, say, cut one's hair. But if this action constitutes dishonesty (e.g., because you have promised to give your hair to someone), it would be objectionable under that description. Furthermore, it seems that if one cuts one hair with the knowledge that this constitutes breaking the given promise, then one's reasons for action do impact the morality of the action. That is, the action is wrong because you are intentionally breaking a promise, and in this case this seems to be your reason for action. So one's reasons for acting may make a morally unobjectionable action wrong. But I do not think this affects the argument we are presently examining. We are considering the case where the reasons for acting do not introduce some further reason for thinking the action wrong.

nuclear strikes for "testing" are wrong, then it seems we must revise our opinion of pre-emptive nuclear strikes generally. If we decide that they require some special reason, or there is no possible justifying reason, then the original supposition that they are morally unproblematic must be abandoned. So, our two actions—pre-emptive nuclear strikes and pre-emptive nuclear strikes to test our capabilities—must stand or fall together.

We may see this last point more clearly by means of a contrastive example. Suppose we are discussing the morality of eating apples. Suppose someone makes the bold claim that eating apples is morally neutral—it is permissible, but neither required nor forbidden. It would be no good to counter such a claim by saying that, if eating apples is morally neutral, then one may eat an apple for any reason whatsoever or for no reason at all. For this is just the point of the original assertion: there is no need for a special reason; "I just felt like it" suffices. Again, note that there are cases where eating an apple might be morally wrong—perhaps the apple is poisoned and you know it, and eating the apple constitutes committing suicide, or perhaps your doctor has told you to limit your sugars and eating an apple violates this command (and you know that it does, and you have a moral obligation to promote your health), or perhaps it is the last bit of food in the house, and you ought to give it to your hungry child—but these are cases where the circumstances have introduced some further reason to not do the action. That is, the action is not wrong under the description "eating an apple," but under some further description—committing suicide, failing to promote one's health, denying one's child nourishment, etc. Under the description "that man is eating an apple" there is no moral question at all; note that this is not the case for the previous example: "That man is performing a pre-emptive nuclear strike" is wrong *under that description.*

So, P seems true, almost tautologous. That is, if permitting x means that we must permit y, then x and y are either both permissible or both impermissible. 6), I contend, follows from this more general principle, and 6) is therefore true. What remains is to find an x and y such that both 4) and 5) come out true. And, as the target of Anscombe's argument is abortion, x will be "abortion." So, it remains to find a suitable "y"—an action that is permissible if abortion generally is permissible, but that is itself a violation of human dignity.

Anscombe suggests the following "y." We would think it wrong—an obvious violation of human dignity—to have an abortion so that one could sell the fetus for medical research (2005, p. 72). Such a case is wrong because it does "commodify"—it treats a human being as though it had merely economic value. This violates human dignity, and thus is wrong. But, Anscombe argues, if we've allowed abortion generally—if we think that abortion is a "neutral" act or even, in some cases, a positive good—we must in principle allow for the financially expedient abortion. If we think there is no reason to object to abortion as such—that is, merely under the description "obtaining an abortion"—then there can be no reason to object to the abortion for financial gain. "For," Anscombe tells us, "you have shewn [sic] the value you set on a human life as such. You are willing to extinguish it as it suits you . . ." (2005, p. 72).

Two principal objections to this reasoning arise. The first is that obtaining an abortion to sell the fetus is not, in fact, wrong. The second objection is that one need not think that abortion is morally "neutral" in the way I have described to think that abortion is permissible in many cases. Thus, our Anscombian argument misses the mark. I shall take up these objections in turn.

First, to trot out an old chestnut, "one philosopher's modus ponens is another's modus tollens." Upon hearing the cases outlined above, one response is to shrug. "Look, it seems a callous thing to do. But if abortion is a morally neutral act—one needs no special reason to obtain one—one can, in fact, do it for reasons we might think frivolous. And, we are committed to the 'neutrality' of abortion, so we simply have a bullet to bite." It seems there are two responses one can make to this objection. One is to cajole one's interlocutor: "you don't *really* think abortion is permissible for financial gain, do you?" The other—more promising—response is to find another action that must be permissible if abortion is generally permissible, and hope that it is more obviously a violation of human dignity.

I shall attempt this latter course. Here is the proposed action: sex-selective abortion. It is common practice in certain parts of the world to value male children much more highly than female ones. Infanticide is often used to accomplish the goal of having a more favorable ratio of male to female children, but parents also use abortion to achieve the desired family composition. This kind of "gendercide" is objectionable, perhaps (hopefully!) obviously so. I think that this too is a violation of human dignity; it fails to respect female human beings as human beings. (Incidentally, it is true that sex-selective abortion causes many societal ills—there are insufficient women for men to marry, a precipitous drop in the birthrate, etc. But to say that one ought not to endorse sex-selective abortion for these reasons strikes me as a grotesque parody of moral reasoning. Sex-selective abortion is wrong in itself, not because of some further consequences.)

But note that if we think of abortion *qua* abortion as morally permissible, then, by our previous reasoning, we must also say that sex-selective abortion is permissible. And, if sex-selective abortion is not permissible because it violates human dignity, then abortion, generally, *cannot* be permissible, for it violates human dignity in the same way that sex-selective abortion does. Again, if we say that the human being itself does not have dignity, and claim that we may kill it in its more undeveloped forms, then it is unclear why we could protest the practice of sex-selective abortion—for there is no human dignity to violate. It sounds like nonsense to say that very early human beings have no human dignity, but it is gravely immoral to treat a subset of them as having no dignity. We may still find sex-selective abortion abhorrent, or socially non-optimal, but we have lost our ability to object to it in a principled way.

The second objection to our argument comes from those defending a more intermediate position on abortion. The objector I have in mind thinks that abortion is morally complex. He will balk *both* at the characterization of abortion as morally neutral, and as something wrong in itself. Many abortions are permissible, this objector claims, but not for the frivolous reasons listed above. But there are many good reasons to abort a pregnancy, which my discussion of Anscombe's argument ignores: what about "therapeutic" abortion, or cases of rape, incest, or severe financial hardship? The objector has a point. It seems that the argument does not work in these cases. Recall that the second premise of the main argument claims that abortion violates human dignity. And to support this claim, I argued that allowing for abortion generally would allow for an abortion in cases that were obviously wrong. But note the objection here: our imagined objector is not attempting defend to abortion generally, but rather abortion in some limited cases. So, trying to fill in premise 4), our x is "abortion for good reason"—and note that we cannot move from allowing this to allowing sex-selective abortion. For, surely, this is not a good reason to abort. The argument I have presented leaves these cases untouched and therefore cannot draw such a sweeping conclusion as it attempts. In other words, if we allow for abortion in some limited cases, then it isn't clear that all abortion violates human dignity.

We might be satisfied even with this limited conclusion. But I want to press back against this objection--to make the strong claim that all abortion violates human dignity. Anscombe herself makes this claim: she is categorical in her rejection of abortion as evil. Let's see what we can make of the objection. It seems there are two kinds of reasons to think an abortion is permissible: abortions for the well being of the mother, and abortions for the well being of the fetus itself. Let's examine abortions for the sake of the mother first.

Some abortions, the claim goes, promote the flourishing of the mother. We can include here abortions for reasons of rape, incest, the mother's health, and the mother's general happiness and flourishing. By this last item, I mean abortion where the mother is in desperate circumstances, be they financial or familial (imagine, for instance, that family that promises to have nothing to do with a woman unless she aborts, or a boyfriend who vows no support for the child, etc.). These do not seem like frivolous reasons for abortion. We cannot infer from these cases that the more objectionable reasons for abortions are any good. At least, that is what the objector claims. But this objection will not do. With respect to the very real circumstances of the "desperation" reasons, these abortions do, in fact, violate human dignity. We can see this is so because if we permit these abortions we must permit sex-selective abortions, which are supposed to be violations of human dignity. For we can easily imagine a situation in which the mother faces a desperate case because the fetus is female: the boyfriend refuses to provide support for a daughter; the family is only interested in a grandson, and the mother will receive financial support just in case she produces male offspring, etc. But if we are indeed opposed to sex-selective abortion, we must be opposed to abortion for these kinds of utilitarian reasons: what if a sex-selective abortion comes out favorably when we calculate the consequences?

But what about the cases of rape, incest, and abortions that are medically necessary (so-called therapeutic abortions)? For these are cases where the mother's very well being is at stake. How is it possible to flourish while carrying the offspring of one's rapist? What about cases of incest (where there is likely an abusive relationship, as well)? What if the pregnancy threatens the mother's health? The difficulty with endorsing abortion in these cases is this: once we have granted that the fetus is a human being with human dignity—and it seems we must, to consistently affirm the immorality of sex-selective abortion—it seems that the interests of the mother are irrelevant to the morality of abortion. Granted that we have two human beings, each with human dignity, abortion is out of the question. For abortion requires us to say that when two human beings have conflicting interests, the stronger killing the weaker is an acceptable resolution. To say that a human being merits death because his life presents (perhaps severe!) difficulties is simply to fail to respect him as a human being—it is to violate human dignity.[5]

But what about abortions that have the best interests of the child in mind? Here I have in mind severe health problems, indicating a short or pain-filled life (or both), or, again, the cases of rape, incest, and severe financial difficult, where these indicate good chances at an unhappy or undesirable life. The idea, then, is that the abortion is the best thing for the fetus itself. Such a judgment is, in effect, a judgment that the fetus's life, such as it is, is not worth living. I find this reasoning unpersuasive. I am not convinced that suicide, based on the premise that life is no longer worth living, is ever the right choice. But I am quite convinced that judging someone else's life to be not worth living—and thus permissible to dispose of—is immoral. This is a violation of human dignity *par excellence*—the idea that we may dispose of a human being

---

[5]Ectopic pregnancy presents an exception. I think that the tag-team of "indirect" abortion and the doctrine of double effect can handle such cases, but I shall not consider the merits of such a response here. I am grateful to C. Vogler for raising this point.

whose life we do not consider worth living fails to respect that human being as an end in himself. (Note also, by parallel reasoning, abortion for the sake of the child could very well be used to justify sex-selective abortion. Perhaps being a woman in a certain society just isn't a life worth living, etc.)

If this reasoning is correct, we have good reason to reject abortion as immoral. We need not appeal to personhood or a Cartesian soul to motivate this claim, and so progress is possible in settling this question. My hope is that this paper has advanced the debate in some small way.

References

Anscombe, G.E.M. (1957) *Intention.* Ithaca, NY: Cornell University Press.

--. (1975). "Contraception and chastity." London: Catholic Truth Society.

--. (2005). "The dignity of the human being." *Human Life, Action, and Ethics.* Mary Geach and Luke Gormally, eds. Exeter: Imprint Academic, 2005.

Garry, A. (1978). "Pornography and respect for women." *Social Theory and Practice,* 4 (4), 395-421.

Kant, I. (1964). *Groundwork of the metaphysics of morals.* (H.J. Paton, Trans.). New York, NY: Harper & Row

Singer, P. (1975). *Animal liberation.* New York, NY: Random House.

8. Anscombe, Human Dignity, and Physical Handicap

David M. DiQuattro

This paper examines G.E.M. Anscombe's "The Dignity of the Human Being" (2005a) in order to see what insights it holds for thinking about handicap in an age of biotechnology. Anscombe wrote a little on handicap, but not as much as she wrote on some other topics related to human dignity. I focus on handicap since, in light of advances in biotechnology, reflection on handicap serves as a good window into how we think about the dignity of the human being. The requirements of respect for human beings with physical handicaps give the lie to some of the ambitions we have for biotechnology. So handicap is a matter of human dignity that is handled extremely inconsistently in the culture. My reflections in this paper are meant to show that Anscombe's treatment of human dignity is highly germane to addressing the dignity of those with handicaps.

In what follows, I canvas some of Anscombe's comments about human dignity and contrast her views with personhood views of human dignity. I argue that personhood views of dignity and consequentialism have the same core problems with respect to how they view the dignity of those with physical handicaps. In this connection, I introduce and discuss the term 'the consequentialist impulse' in order to capture the role consequentialist reasoning plays in the culture. After critiquing personhood views of dignity and consequentialism with respect to physical handicap, I move on to a discussion of genetic testing. I outline how consequentialist reasoning can be applied to all manner of genetic knowledge – not just knowledge about identifiable handicaps. I do this in order to argue that the prevalence of the consequentialist impulse threatens to erode the dignity of all human beings, not just the dignity of those with identifiable handicaps.

1. Anscombe on Human Dignity

Anscombe said the following about human dignity. "There is just one impregnable equality of all human beings. It lies in the value and dignity of being a human being" (Anscombe, 2005a, p. 67). Anscombe's point was that simply being a human being *all by itself* is the source of the fundamental respect owed to a human being. Anscombe did not *define* the value involved or the respect it entails, but she provided a sense of what is involved by example. She contrasted vengeful killing with the thought that the person *deserved it* with killing for convenience. She wrote,

> To regard someone as deserving death is very definitely regarding him, not just as a human being but as endued with a dignity belonging to human beings, as having free will and as answerable for his actions. I am not defending the murderer I am imagining. He has not the right to kill his victim. But I am *contrasting* him with the murderer who is willing to kill someone for gain or other

> advantage…*He* is not respecting in his victim the dignity of a human being at all. Similarly with 'active euthanasia' which is non-voluntary on the part of the victim. He is to be killed because of the 'disvalue' of his life; his living is of negative value and so things are better with him dead. (Anscombe, 2005a, pp. 68-69)

Anscombe thought it is a violation of human dignity to weigh up the value of a human life against other goods. The dignity of the human being is such that the goods of a human's life cannot be weighed in that way. The value of the human being is 'incomparably higher'[1] and thus cannot be brought into any consequentialist calculus.

Anscombe's comment suggests that we cannot treat a human being's life as just one more value to be weighed because we are *answerable* to other human beings and they are responsible to us and for their actions. So we must not treat others as objects simply to be used for our ends but as subjects to which our actions must be justifiable.

Anscombe affirmed the dignity of every *human being* rather than every *person*. On typical accounts that distinguish human beings and persons, persons must *exhibit* (not just have the capacity to develop) many of the characteristic powers of human beings to a fairly high degree, including complex reasoning and linguistic ability.[2] So on this kind of account, the unborn (and young children) have not yet met the criteria for being a person, while many aged lose their personhood, and seriously mentally handicapped human beings are incapable of becoming persons. Typically, these views claim that dignity, in the sense that Anscombe intends the term, attaches mainly to *persons* rather than to all human beings.

Anscombe (2008c) characterized the view that distinguishes persons and human beings thus:

---

[1]This phrase is from Charles Taylor (1989).

[2]The classic statement of this kind of view is in Warren (1973).

> A human being comes to be a person through the development of the characteristics which make something into a person. A human being in decay may also cease to be a person without ceasing to be a human being. In short: being a person is something that gets added to being a human being who develops properly, and that may disappear in old age and imbecility. (pp. 66-67)

Anscombe listed this view as one of twenty opinions common among Anglo-American philosophers. She commented on all twenty as follows:

> A seriously believing Christian ought not, in my opinion, believe any of them … In saying these opinions are inimical to the Christian religion I am not implying that they can only be judged false on that ground. Each of them is a philosophical error and can be argued to be such on purely philosophical grounds. (Anscombe, 2008c, pp. 66, 68)

Anscombe's criterion for possession of human dignity was a *biological criterion* – being a member of the human species is sufficient to possess the special value and dignity discussed above. Anscombe understood the identity of human beings in Aristotelian/Thomistic terms (Anscombe, 2008a).

Insofar as personhood views deny what Anscombe considers the one impregnable equality of all human beings, these views undermine absolute prohibitions about the treatment of human beings based on this impregnable equality. Insofar as personhood views undermine such prohibitions, Anscombe's disagreement with such views will closely parallel her disagreements with consequentialism. I wish to treat these two views (personhood views of dignity on the one hand and consequentialism on the other) in tandem in order to bring out the insights Anscombe's work holds for thinking about physical handicap and genetic testing.

Anscombe had a lot to say about consequentialist reasoning and its manifestations in the culture. I will say a few words about that in order to introduce the phrase 'the consequentialist impulse' and to explain what I mean by the phrase. The below comments will also help explain my reasoning that the personhood account of dignity and consequentialism have the same core problems with respect to human frailty and handicap.

2. The Consequentialist Impulse

Anscombe identified characteristic modes of reasoning in both philosophical and cultural discourse that lend support to consequentialism. These modes of reasoning consider some purported specifically wrong action type (e.g. securing the judicial execution of the innocent) and seek to find an (often outlandish) example where it would be permissible or even required to perform that type of action (Anscombe, 1958; Anscombe, 2005b).

Below, I provide a characterization of how consequentialist reasoning works. I imagine an argument about the justification of torture and enhanced interrogation methods. Justifications of torture often proceed by discussing extreme cases. For example, a bomb is ticking in Midtown New York, and you have detained the only person who knows the code to disarm the bomb, but he won't talk. Is it permissible to use torture if that is the only way to save millions of lives? [3]

Consider a debate between two interlocutors, one opposed to the CIA's program of enhanced interrogation methods to deal with terrorism, and the other not opposed. The person opposed to the CIA's program argues that it used torture and that torture is a bad sort of thing to do, and always wrong. His interlocutor provides the ticking time bomb example that

[3] I am mainly speaking of discussions in popular discourse. I do not claim that ticking bomb cases are used this way in academic discussions.

tries to show that torture would be permissible in that case. Perhaps the CIA critic might circumscribe his formulation of the prohibition against torture. For example, he could re-describe the prohibition thus: 'it is always wrong to torture in such and such a way.' He could then argue that the CIA program violated *that* prohibition. But his interlocutor can provide a counterexample to the principle so circumscribed and so on. Notice, to this point the defender of torture has not *directly* defended the actual procedures of the CIA. He or she has only provided counterexamples to proposed prohibitions related to torture.

After a few rounds of this kind of discussion, you can imagine the CIA defender reasoning with his interlocutor as follows:

> "Look, you are not going to get very far trying to say that the CIA interrogation techniques were bad sorts of things to do, because we can always find an instance where a supposed bad type of action is permissible. There is a problem with the notion of avoiding 'bad kinds of action.' The problem is that you think people need to keep their hands clean by not intentionally doing base sorts of actions in horrible circumstances. And you say that if even *worse* things happen as a result of the person being unwilling to get his hands dirty, so be it. You want people to be able to claim *innocence* because of the intentional actions they avoid. But I've cast doubt on the idea that there are these 'base kinds of actions.' So there isn't a basis for your scruple that there are certain things you 'just shouldn't do.' Since that is the case, the impression of maintaining innocence by avoiding such actions is illusory. There is no escaping responsibility for what happens just because you avoided performing a supposedly base action. You have to take responsibility for everything that came of your actions and omissions

> and for everything that could have been avoided if you were willing to get over your misplaced scruples about things you 'just shouldn't do.'"[4]

Notice the result of this kind of reasoning. It calls into question whether the nature and quality of one's act is relevant to determining its permissibility. The above reasoning undermines the following kind of thought: "normally I would think it is good to avoid torture, but I suppose certain factors *could* outweigh the reasons not to engage in that action which is normally wrong." Consequentialist reasoning undermines the idea that it would require extreme or dire circumstances to override a normally prohibited action. It does so by arguing that there is no *special* reason not to do *that kind of thing* since the nature and quality of your action is irrelevant to your guilt or responsibility. The reason certain actions are normally wrong has nothing to do with the intrinsic quality of the action, but with *other* factors regarding what comes of the action.[5] So this reasoning allows one to justify torture in cases very different and less extreme than the examples the CIA defender cites. As long as what comes of the action is better than what you gain by avoiding torture, you are justified in using torture.

This kind of reasoning is 'indefinitely applicable.' Since the reasoning above seeks to undermine the legitimacy of *any* reasoning based on the intrinsic quality of an action it is indefinitely applicable in two ways. First, it can be applied to any action type to try to show that actions falling under that type are not always wrong. Second, it can be used over and over again in order to undermine the general claim that some actions are prohibited because of the kinds of actions they are.

---

[4]In this paragraph, I have drawn heavily on Anscombe's assessment (2005b) of how the culture and modern moral philosophy conceive of issues of responsibility and prohibition.

[5]To be precise, the intrinsic nature can be relevant only insofar as it is an aspect of the overall state of affairs that an action brings about.

This ability to indefinitely apply consequentialist reasoning is crucial to how the consequentialist impulse functions in the culture. Anscombe (1958) diagnosed how consequentialist argument and the use of examples functioned in the culture:

> The point of considering hypothetical situations, perhaps very improbable ones, seems to be to elicit from yourself or someone else a hypothetical decision to do something of a bad kind. I don't doubt this has the effect of predisposing people - who will never get into the situations for which they have made hypothetical choices - to consent to similar bad actions, or to praise and flatter those who do them, so long as their crowd does so too, when the desperate circumstances imagined don't hold at all. (p. 13)

One justifies doing a certain type of action in extreme circumstances. As I showed above, this kind of argument erodes confidence in the importance of the nature and quality of actions, so the idea that an act is bad presents no resistance to overriding considerations. We can see how this provides a formula for rationalizing bad actions in mundane circumstances when there is something (anything) to be gained from the bad action. Anscombe thought that the consequentialist impulse provided rationalizations for conventionally approved bad actions that have nothing to do with the consequentialist's extreme examples.[6] For convenience and vividness, I will speak below of 'slippage' between justifying an action type in extreme circumstances, and using that justification to justify the action type in more mundane circumstances.

---

[6]See Anscombe, 1958, p. 13 for Anscombe's assessment of the conventional respectability of the prescriptions to be found in modern moral philosophy. See also Anscombe, 2005b.

This tendency to slip from extreme examples to justifying the type of action being considered in non-extreme cases is important for the concerns I raise about genetic testing. But first I turn to a more general critique of personhood views of dignity and consequentialism with respect to physical handicap.

3. Personhood Views of Dignity and Human Handicap

Personhood views of dignity and consequentialism have the same core problems with respect to how they view the dignity of those with physical handicaps.[7] In this section I will focus on these problems with respect to personhood views of dignity. According to standard personhood views of dignity, seriously mentally handicapped humans do not satisfy the personhood standard, and hence do not possess the same dignity as other human beings. And I will suggest that employing a personhood standard of dignity also erodes our honoring the dignity of those with handicaps who *do* satisfy that standard.

Many individuals with physical handicaps reach (currently defended) thresholds for personhood. So according to these personhood accounts they possess human dignity. But this reasoning shows precisely what is wrong with a personhood account of dignity: it gives us, to adapt Bernard Williams's phrase (1981), 'one thought too many' about a human being's dignity. According to personhood accounts, a (not too seriously) handicapped person has dignity because he

---

[7]Throughout this section I mean the phrase 'those with physical handicaps' to also cover those with mental handicaps, since human mental handicaps are either physical conditions or inextricably tied up with our physicality.

is a human being *and* his handicap is not too serious.[8] But the second part of that reasoning (the handicap is not too serious) is exactly the wrong thought with respect to physical handicaps. Consider how this view would have us construe the reasons for caring for the physical needs of someone with a physical handicap. It would not be sufficient to say we care for those with handicaps because they need it. Instead, we would need to construe our reasons thus: we care for the physical needs of those with handicaps because they need it *and their need is not serious enough to render them not a person.*

But if personhood reasoning gives us one thought too many about the dignity of those with handicaps, it gives us one thought too many about *everyone's* dignity. On the personhood view, the conditions for *anyone* having dignity are not just that she is a human being but also that she has sufficiently developed capacities and hasn't suffered trauma or aging to such an extent that it has removed her personhood. Anscombe (2005a) raised this problem well. She wrote:

> This lack of reverence, of respect for that dignity of human nature so wonderfully created by God, is lack of regard for the one impregnable equality of all human beings. Lacking it, you cannot revere the dignity of your own human-ness, that is the dignity of that same human nature in yourself. You may value yourself highly as a

---

[8]To be fair, many personhood accounts lend no special significance to being a human being that provides a presumption of respect over other species. On that kind of view, I have to admit that proponents don't want us to have one thought too many about dignity, but instead want us to have the *wrong thought*. They don't want parents of a seriously handicapped child to have the thought 'this is my child, so I will care for it'; they want them to have the thought 'this child who is mine does not have a handicap serious enough to render it not a person, so I will care for it.' Williams's 'one thought too many' phrase is still helpful here because it draws our attention to the fact that an idea *intrudes* into our deliberations that should not be there, even if we do not act badly in response to the idea.

> tennis player or a natural scientist, but without a change of heart you cannot value yourself as being a human, a Mensch. For you have shewn the value you set on a human life as such. You are willing to extinguish it as suits you or as suits the people who want you to do so. (p. 72)

Personhood views not only give one thought too many about the dignity of those with handicaps. They also misunderstand the ways in which handicaps contribute to human dignity. Consider someone with a mental disorder that nonetheless crosses the threshold of mental capacity to be a person according to the standard account. Someone with the personhood view has to see that person's disability as presenting a threat to her personhood that nonetheless hasn't managed to prevent her from being a person. The best gloss on this is to say that according to a standard personhood view she is a person *despite* her handicap. This is exactly the wrong way to think of those with handicaps. It fails to see the dignity and value in the way those with handicaps 'stick themselves into the world'[9] in ways that negotiate the challenges of doing so. Indeed, the personhood view fails to properly appreciate the centrality to human life of negotiating the weakness, frailties, and challenges we face as embodied beings in a physical world.[10]

4. Personhood, Consequentialism, and Handicap

Both the personhood account of dignity and consequentialism have the same problem regarding dignity, and the problem comes into stark relief when thinking about physical handicap.

---

[9]I owe this phrase to H. Collin Messer.

[10]This is not to say that doing this well is a *condition* of an individual possessing the value and dignity of a human being. It is simply to say that this sort of thing is so tied up with the human 'form of life' that it is impossible to understand the value of human life without taking adequate stock of this.

Because of their physical infirmities, those with handicaps have a *harder* time than others showing that they pass muster to not have their persons and bodies violated for some end. We have seen how this works in the case of the personhood view of dignity. But the same structure holds for consequentialism. Many people with handicaps *in virtue of their handicaps* are less capable than they would be without their handicap of enjoying and producing whatever good end a given consequentialist view claims we ought to maximize. Insofar as that is the case, on a consequentialist view, it is easier to justify actions toward them that would normally count as violations of dignity for the sake of good ends to be enjoyed by others who do not share these infirmities.

The core problem with personhood accounts of dignity and consequentialism is that the most vulnerable typically count less in deliberations about how to act toward others, which is exactly the opposite of what respect for human beings demands. But the problem does not show up as starkly in issues like active euthanasia or abortion. In the case of active euthanasia, the act is ostensibly done to ease the suffering of the person who is killed. Abortion presents the complexities of the mother's bodily integrity. Thinking about handicap shows us the problem clearly. I think it is clear that these views lead us to think about handicap in exactly the wrong way. The idea of human dignity does not place a *higher* burden on those with infirmities to justify their rights not to be violated. The idea of human dignity is that we are *protected* regardless of our infirmities from those who would exploit or violate us for some end.

Below I consider the relevance of all of this for thinking about genetic testing. Testing has become an integral part of bringing children into the world. Testing, particularly genetic testing, means greater awareness not only about genuine handicaps and disorders but of all manner of frailties, disease proclivities, and potential problems for future offspring (e.g.

if a tested child has an allele for a disorder inherited in a recessive pattern).

The knowledge gained by testing is highly problematic in a culture where the consequentialist impulse and personhood standards of dignity hold sway in the way that they do. Testing allows us to identify a host of ways in which a person's life (or the lives of their potential offspring) could be compromised as a result of the person's genetic makeup. As our ability to detect these potential problems increases along with our ability to reduce the incidence of people born with these problems – through selective abortion and genetic engineering – I think the following will happen (and is happening): all manner of genetic anomalies, deficiencies, and potential problems will be handled the same way that physical handicap is treated in the culture. And I have argued that physical handicap is handled quite badly indeed. The point is that *all* or *most* children will have to grow up in and learn to negotiate a world in which knowledge of their various genetic frailties is readily available and where these genetic frailties are handled in a manner inconsistent with human dignity.

In raising concerns about genetic testing, I wish to highlight the broader cultural context, influenced by the consequentialist impulse, in which testing takes place. My concern is connected to the indefinite applicability of consequentialist reasoning which I spoke about above. I want to suggest how the indefinite applicability of consequentialist reasoning can interact with the kind of knowledge that pre-natal genetic testing provides. The comprehensiveness of the genetic information available through genetic testing allows that knowledge to interact with the consequentialist impulse in problematic ways. The phenomenon of 'slippage' is important here.

One can see the rationale for wanting to test for serious illnesses and anomalies such as cystic fibrosis or Down syndrome, even if selective abortion is not on the table. There is potentially important knowledge gained that can prepare parents for the care their child might require. However, consider a genetically tested fetus that does not have cystic fibrosis, but is determined to be a carrier of the disease. Such testing can seem innocuous, because this information will have very little effect on how this fetus is treated throughout its life. However, consequentialist reasoning allows us to find an extreme example where, e.g., aborting a fetus simply because it is a carrier for a disease seems justified. Again, the next step is to argue that the extreme example shows that there can be no special reason not to abort such fetuses, rooted in the dignity of the human being or because of the kind of action aborting would be. The reasons not to abort would have to be reasons of a different kind, and they would have to be weighed up against countervailing reasons.

The ability to apply this reasoning to any type of action is what interests me in connection with the comprehensive information that genetic testing makes available. It makes it possible for us to zero in on any piece of genetic information and justify genetic engineering, selective abortion and other means of combating or eradicating that genetic feature. Further, the indefinite applicability of consequentialist reasoning and its influence in the culture means that there can be a certain arbitrariness to which traits are focused on – there is a consequentialist rationale available for combating or eliminating just about any trait. That is why I suggested above that the problem could become *widespread*, where most people have at least some known traits that are viewed as sub-optimal, and for which some consequentialist justification regarding combating or eliminating the trait has been canvased.

5. Conclusion

I close with a quote from one of Anscombe's recently published lectures followed by a few comments on the quote. Anscombe (Anscombe, 2008b) writes:

> To quote Scripture: 'The tender mercies of the wicked are cruel'. Remember that we have just been celebrating one of those 'Years' that are announced nowadays: the 'Year of the Disabled'. And one of the ways in which we celebrated it in this country was to have the green light given to people who want to kill babies that their parents don't want ... That is the situation we are in; and we ought to regard ourselves, as we do not, I fear, as separate. (p. 116)

"That is the situation we are in; and we ought to regard ourselves, as we do not, I fear, as separate." Anscombe chides us for our naïveté about the world we live in and its proneness to disregard and abuse human dignity, sometimes in the name of humanitarian ends ("the tender mercies of the wicked are cruel"). My argument is that dominant cultural conceptions of the basis for human dignity are unable to deal adequately with human frailty or handicap. And Anscombe's writings show us how deeply the mistakes in reasoning and sensibilities run in the culture. Her comment that we do not regard ourselves as separate invites us to consider the ways we are entrenched in that culture. It seems that it is especially important to consider the ways it will be necessary to not be entrenched in the culture of genetic testing as it currently exists and is likely to develop.[11]

---

[11]This comment does not imply that there can be no place for genetic testing. My argument concerns the overall context in which genetic testing is practiced, not the permissibility of testing in any circumstances.

References

Anscombe, G.E.M. (1958). Modern Moral Philosophy. *Philosophy* , *33* (124), 1-19.

Anscombe, G.E.M. (2005a). The Dignity of the Human Being. In G.E.M. Anscombe, *Human Life, Action and Ethics* (pp. 67-76). M. Geach, & L. Gormally (Eds.). Exeter: Imprint Academic.

Anscombe, G.E.M. (2005b). Does Oxford Moral Philosophy Corrupt Youth. In G.E.M. Anscombe, *Human Life, Action and Ethics* (pp. 161-168). M. Geach, & L. Gormally (Eds.). Exeter: Imprint Academic.

Anscombe, G.E.M. (2008a). The Early Embryo: Theoretical Doubts and Practical Certainties. In G.E.M. Anscombe, *Faith in a Hard Ground* (pp. 214-223). M. Geach, & L. Gormally (Eds.). Exeter: Imprint Academic.

Anscombe, G.E.M. (2008b). Morality. In G.E.M. Anscombe, *Faith in a Hard Ground* (pp. 113-116). M. Geach, & L. Gormally (Eds.). Exeter: Imprint Academic.

Anscombe, G.E.M. (2008c). Twenty Opinions Common Among Anglo-American Philosophers. In G.E.M. Anscombe, *Faith in a Hard Ground* (pp. 66-68). M. Geach, & L. Gormally (Eds.). Exeter: Imprint Academic.

Taylor, C. (1989). *Sources of the Self.* Cambridge, MA: Harvard University Press.

Warren, M. A. (1973). The Moral and Legal Status of Abortion. *The Monist, 57* (1), 43-61.

Williams, B. (1981). Persons, Character and Morality. In B. Williams, *Moral Luck* (pp. 1-19). Cambridge: Cambridge University Press.

Contributors

RYAN COBB is a philosophy graduate student at the University of Iowa.

T.A. CAVANAUGH is Professor of Philosophy at the University of San Francisco.

DAVID DIQUATTRO is a Philosophy Adjunct Instructor at Stetson University.

DAVID B. HERSHENOV is Professor of Philosophy and Department Chair, at the University at Buffalo.

JOHN MIZZONI is Professor of Philosophy and Head of the Department of Arts & Humanities at Neumann University.

BRYAN C. PILKINGTON is Assistant Professor of Philosophy at Aquinas College.

DUNCAN RICHTER is Professor of English, Rhetoric, & Humanistic Studies at the Virginia Military Institute.

CANDACE VOGLER is the David B. and Clara E. Stern Professor of Philosophy at the University of Chicago.

www.ingramcontent.com/pod-product-compliance
Lightning Source LLC
Chambersburg PA
CBHW021403090426
42742CB00009B/979
* 9 7 8 1 9 4 4 7 6 9 1 6 1 *